# GREAT GRAPH ART

## Multiplication & Division

### by Cindi Mitchell

S C H O L A S T I C
**PROFESSIONAL BOOKS**

**New York** ◆ **Toronto** ◆ **London** ◆ **Auckland** ◆ **Sydney**
**New Delhi** ◆ **Mexico City** ◆ **Hong Kong**

To my mother, Dorothy Neibler,
who always encouraged me to hitch my wagon to a star.

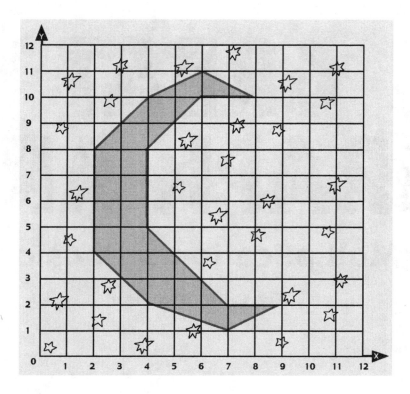

Cover and interior design by Pamela Simmons
Interior illustrations by Kate Flanagan

ISBN 0-590-64374-6
Copyright © 1999 by Cindi Mitchell

# CONTENTS

# INTRODUCTION

Mathematics is the foundation for creating many forms of art, such as kaleidoscopes, quilts, tapestries, weavings, and graphic designs. This book was created to give children opportunities to use mathematics to create art in the form of graphs.

Your students will enjoy plotting the points and connecting them to create delightful pictures. In the process, they will learn a lot about graphing, multiplication, and division. In addition, they will discover that math is more than basic computation—in fact, math is about creativity, art, and fun! Here's how it works.

### How to Use This Book

Each activity consists of two pages, a graph page and a worksheet of math problems. First, students read a riddle at the top of the graph page. For example, the riddle for The Silent Phone Mystery (pages 57–58) poses the question, *What kind of phone never rings?* Students then look at the corresponding page of instructions and solve the division problems to find number pairs. They then plot the number pairs, in order, on the graph. When they connect the points, they complete a design, and the picture is the solution to the riddle. In this activity, students plot and connect points to make a saxophone. The phone that never rings is a saxophone!

For students who are just beginning to learn multiplication and division facts, allow two days to complete each activity. On the first day, have students solve the

multiplication or division problems. The following day let them plot the points, create the picture, and solve the riddle!

Each activity also includes an Extra Challenge! problem. These silly riddles, wacky games, and mathematical rebuses will amaze and amuse even the most reluctant mathematician.

### How to Begin

Choose one or two activities to introduce and teach coordinate graphing. Then use the others to reinforce multiplication and division facts, or use the activities to teach a unit on graphing. The skill focus of each activity appears at the top of each activity page. You'll also find the math skills listed in progressive level of difficulty in the Contents on page 3.

### Taking It Further

After students have finished graphing the pictures, have them add their personal, creative touch by coloring them with crayons or colored pencils. Invite them to add drawings in the foreground and background or enhance the pictures by adding to them. For instance, they may add ornaments to the tree (Out on a Limb, pages 47–48), or draw the "man in the moon" (Funny Money, pages 55–56). Display the picture graphs in a prominent place in your classroom.

Use the activities in this book to encourage your students to come up with their own sets of math problems and accompanying graph pictures for classmates to solve and create. Have fun!

— Cindi Mitchell

Name_____

# CAT DETECTIVE

**What was the cat detective looking for?**_____

To find out the answer, solve the problems on page 6. Then plot the number pairs and connect the points. The picture you make will help you solve the riddle. (The answer is upside down at the bottom of this page.)

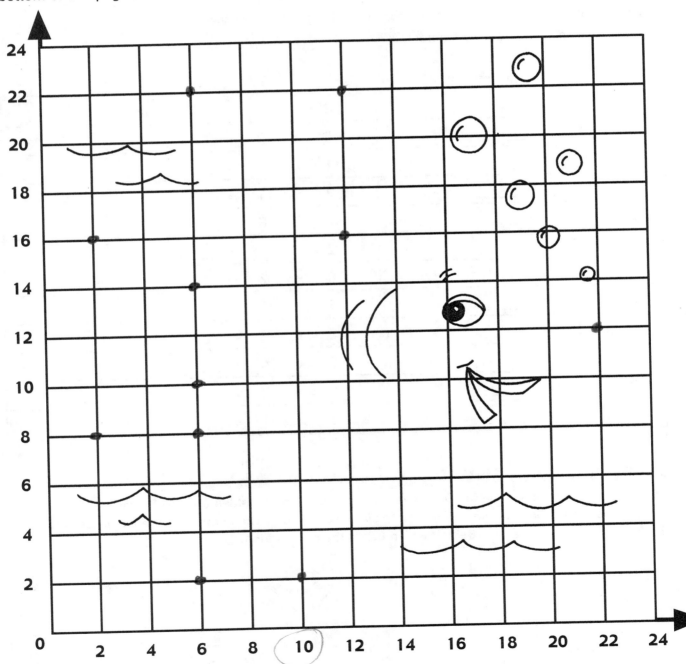

Answer: **something fishy**

Name_____

# CAT DETECTIVE

**1.** Solve each multiplication problem. Example problems have been done for you.

**2.** In the example problems, the numbers **10** and **2** are called a number pair. We write (10, 2).

**3.** Look at the graph on page 5. Graph the number pairs in the example. Start at 0.
Go across to the number **10** and up to the number **2**. Plot the point.

**4.** Plot the point for each number pair. Then use a straightedge to connect the points in the order you plotted them. Can you solve the riddle?

X ⟶        Y ↑

| | |
|---|---|
| 2 x 5 = 10 | 2 x 1 = 2 (Example) |
| 2 x 11 = _____ | 6 x 2 = _____ |
| 5 x 2 = _____ | 11 x 2 = _____ |
| 2 x 3 = _____ | 2 x 11 = _____ |
| 2 x 6 = _____ | 2 x 8 = _____ |
| 2 x 3 = _____ | 2 x 7 = _____ |
| 2 x 1 = _____ | 8 x 2 = _____ |
| 1 x 2 = _____ | 4 x 2 = _____ |
| 3 x 2 = _____ | 5 x 2 = _____ |
| 6 x 2 = _____ | 2 x 4 = _____ |
| 2 x 3 = _____ | 1 x 2 = _____ |
| 5 x 2 = _____ | 2 x 1 = _____ |

## EXTRA CHALLENGE!

Thanks to his sharp eyes, the Cat Detective found a "fishy" note hidden under a flowerpot. It read: *The gold is hidden behind one of the fish tiles in the bathroom.* The number on the fish is less than 9 x 2, and it is a multiple of 2. Behind which fish is the gold hidden?_____

12   15   50   3   11   20   7   1

*Great Graph Art: Multiplication & Division Scholastic Professional Books*

Name_____

# CUPID'S VISIT

**Why did Cupid visit the tailor ?** _____

To find out the answer, solve the problems on page 8. Then plot the number pairs and connect the points. The picture you make will help you solve the riddle. (The answer is upside down at the bottom of this page.)

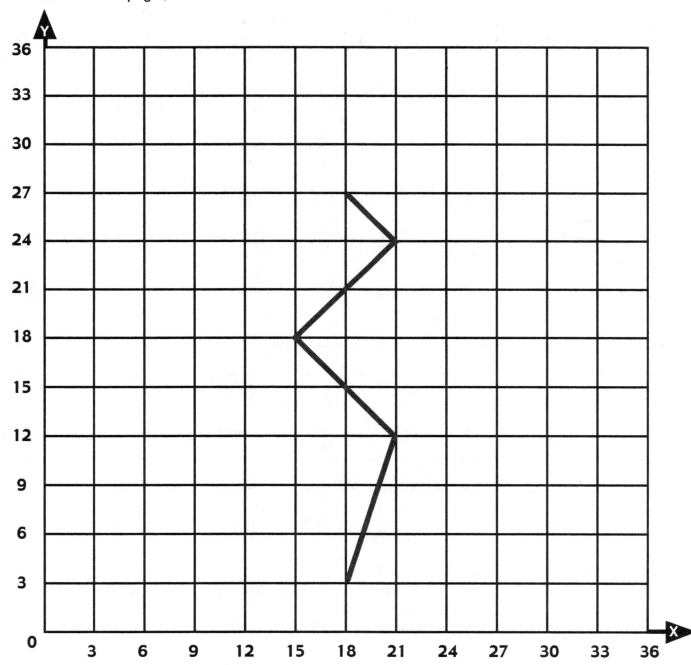

Answer: He wanted help mending broken hearts.

# CUPID'S VISIT

**1.** Solve each multiplication problem. Example problems have been done for you.

**2.** In the example problems, the numbers **18** and **3** are called a number pair. We write (18, 3).

**3.** Look at the graph on page 7. Graph the number pairs in the example. Start at 0.
Go across to the number **18** and up to the number **3**. Plot the point.

**4.** Plot the point for each number pair, in order  Then use a straightedge to connect the points in the order you plotted them. Can you solve the riddle?

| X ⟶ | | | | Y ↑ | | | |
|---|---|---|---|---|---|---|---|
| 3 | x | 6 | = 18 | 1 | x | 3 | = 3 (Example) |
| 3 | x | 7 | = _____ | 3 | x | 2 | = _____ |
| 3 | x | 9 | = _____ | 3 | x | 4 | = _____ |
| 3 | x | 11 | = _____ | 6 | x | 3 | = _____ |
| 11 | x | 3 | = _____ | 9 | x | 3 | = _____ |
| 10 | x | 3 | = _____ | 3 | x | 11 | = _____ |
| 3 | x | 8 | = _____ | 11 | x | 3 | = _____ |
| 3 | x | 6 | = _____ | 9 | x | 3 | = _____ |
| 4 | x | 3 | = _____ | 11 | x | 3 | = _____ |
| 3 | x | 2 | = _____ | 3 | x | 11 | = _____ |
| 3 | x | 1 | = _____ | 9 | x | 3 | = _____ |
| 1 | x | 3 | = _____ | 6 | x | 3 | = _____ |
| 3 | x | 3 | = _____ | 4 | x | 3 | = _____ |
| 5 | x | 3 | = _____ | 2 | x | 3 | = _____ |
| 3 | x | 6 | = _____ | 3 | x | 1 | = _____ |

# EXTRA CHALLENGE!

Silly Sam bought Gretchen a box of chocolates for Valentine's Day. There was only one problem. When Gretchen opened the box of candy she noticed that every third piece was missing. If there were 12 pieces of candy left in the box, how many did Silly Sam take out?
(Hint: It will help to draw a picture.) _____

Great Graph Art: Multiplication & Division Scholastic Professional Books

# PET STORE

**What kind of animal did the bald man buy at the pet store?**_____

To find out the answer, solve the problems on page 10. Then plot the number pairs and connect the points. The picture you make will help you solve the riddle. (The answer is upside down at the bottom of this page.)

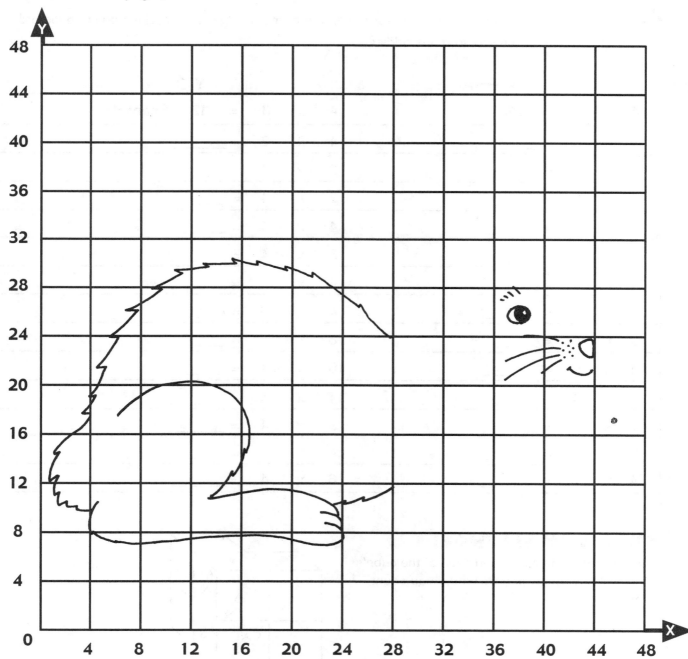

Answer: **A rabbit. He wanted some hair (hare).**

# PET STORE

**1.** Solve each multiplication problem. Example problems have been done for you.

**2.** In the example problems, the numbers **28** and **12** are called a number pair. We write (28, 12).

**3.** Look at the graph on page 9. Graph the number pairs in the example. Start at 0.
Go across to the number **28** and up to the number **12**. Plot the point.

**4.** Plot the point for each number pair, in order. Then use a straightedge to connect the points in the order you plotted them. Can you solve the riddle?

| X ⟶ | | | | Y ↑ | | | |
|---|---|---|---|---|---|---|---|
| 4 x 7 = 28 | | | | 4 x 3 = 12 (Example) | | | |
| 4 x 8 = _____ | | | | 4 x 2 = _____ | | | |
| 8 x 5 = _____ | | | | 2 x 4 = _____ | | | |
| 4 x 9 = _____ | | | | 3 x 4 = _____ | | | |
| 4 x 10 = _____ | | | | 4 x 4 = _____ | | | |
| 10 x 4 = _____ | | | | 5 x 4 = _____ | | | |
| 11 x 4 = _____ | | | | 4 x 5 = _____ | | | |
| 4 x 11 = _____ | | | | 4 x 6 = _____ | | | |
| 9 x 4 = _____ | | | | 8 x 4 = _____ | | | |
| 4 x 9 = _____ | | | | 10 x 4 = _____ | | | |
| 8 x 4 = _____ | | | | 11 x 4 = _____ | | | |
| 7 x 4 = _____ | | | | 9 x 4 = _____ | | | |
| 8 x 4 = _____ | | | | 4 x 7 = _____ | | | |
| 4 x 7 = _____ | | | | 6 x 4 = _____ | | | |

## EXTRA CHALLENGE!

If you counted the carrots on each of the cube's six faces, how many carrots would you count in all?_____

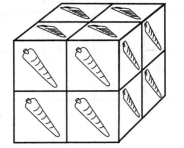

*Great Graph Art: Multiplication & Division Scholastic Professional Books*

# ALPHABET

**I start with an "e" and have only one letter. What am I?** _____

To find out the answer, solve the problems on page 12. Then plot the number pairs and connect the points. The picture you make will help you solve the riddle. (The answer is upside down at the bottom of this page.)

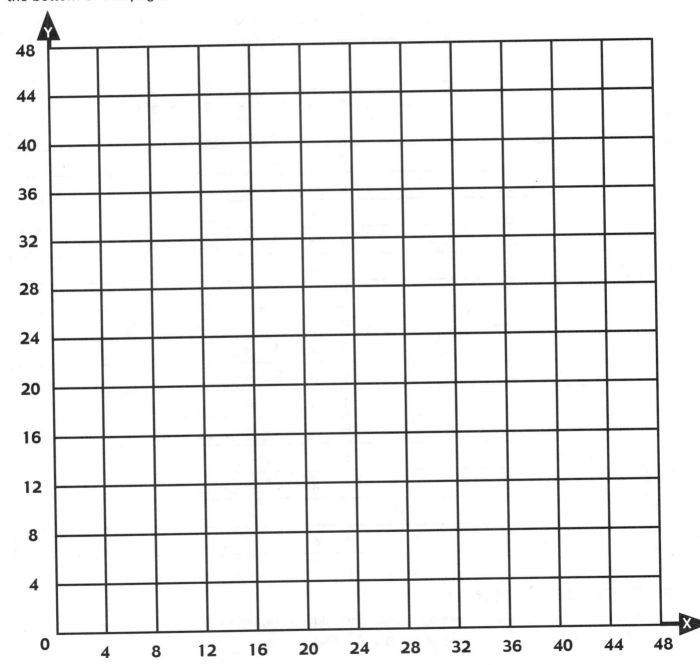

Answer: an envelope

**Name** _Justin_

# ALPHABET

**1.** Solve each multiplication problem. Example problems have been done for you.

**2.** In the example problems, the numbers **4** and **8** are called a number pair. We write (4, 8).

**3.** Look at the graph on page 11. Graph the number pairs in the example. Start at 0.
Go across to the number **4** and up to the number **8**. Plot the point.

**4.** Plot the point for each number pair, in order. Then use a straightedge to connect the points in the order you plotted them. After the word STOP, start a new line. Can you solve the riddle?

**X** ⟶                                         **Y** ⬆

| | | | | | | | | | |
|---|---|---|---|---|---|---|---|---|---|
| 1 x 4 = 4 | | | | | 2 x 4 = 8 (Example) | | | | |
| 11 x 4 = _____ | | | | | 2 x 4 = _____ | | | | |
| 4 x 11 = _____ | | | | | 9 x 4 = _____ | | | | |
| 1 x 4 = _____ | | | | | 4 x 9 = _____ | | | | |
| 4 x 1 = _____ | | | | | 4 x 2 = _____ | | | | |
| 4 x 2 = _____ | | | | | 4 x 3 = _____ | | | | |
| 3 x 4 = _____ | | | | | 4 x 4 = _____ | | | | |
| 4 x 4 = _____ | | | | | 4 x 5 = _____ | | | | |
| 5 x 4 = _____ | | | | | 6 x 4 = _____ STOP | | | | |
| 4 x 1 = _____ | | | | | 9 x 4 = _____ | | | | |
| 4 x 6 = _____ | | | | | 4 x 5 = _____ | | | | |
| 11 x 4 = _____ | | | | | 4 x 9 = _____ STOP | | | | |
| 4 x 7 = _____ | | | | | 6 x 4 = _____ | | | | |
| 4 x 8 = _____ | | | | | 5 x 4 = _____ | | | | |
| 9 x 4 = _____ | | | | | 4 x 4 = _____ | | | | |
| 10 x 4 = _____ | | | | | 4 x 3 = _____ | | | | |
| 4 x 11 = _____ | | | | | 4 x 2 = _____ | | | | |

## EXTRA CHALLENGE!

What letter never gets put in an envelope? Solve the riddle by replacing the answers to the problems with the alphabet code.

E = 12    B = 16    A = 20

4 x 5 = ___ ☐      4 x 4 = ___ ☐      4 x 3 = ___ ☐      3 x 4 = ___ ☐

Great Graph Art: Multiplication & Division Scholastic Professional Books

# OUTER SPACE

**What kind of fish likes to study outer space?** _____

To find out the answer, solve the problems on page 14. Then plot the number pairs and connect the points. The picture you make will help you solve the riddle. (The answer is upside down at the bottom of this page.)

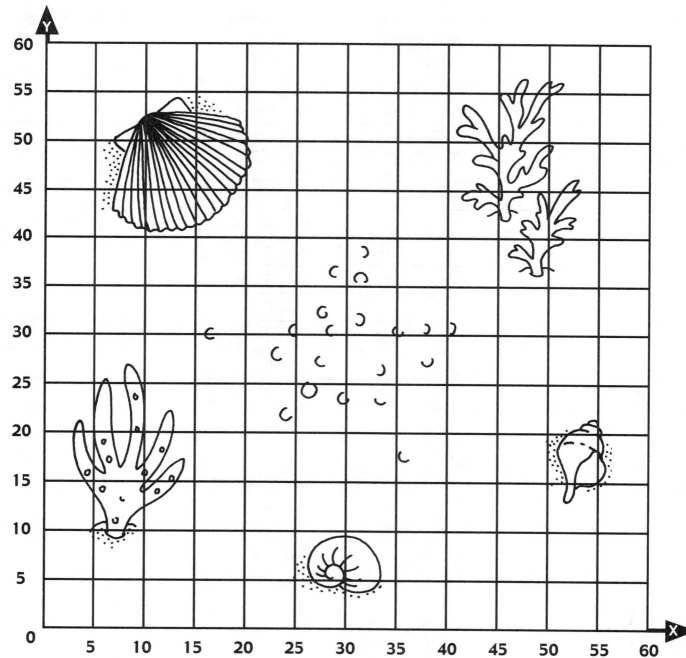

Great Graph Art: Multiplication & Division Scholastic Professional Books

13

# OUTER SPACE

**1.** Solve each multiplication problem. Example problems have been done for you.

**2.** In the example problems, the numbers **30** and **55** are called a number pair. We write (30, 55).

**3.** Look at the graph on page 13. Graph the number pairs in the example. Start at 0.
Go across to the number **30** and up to the number **55**. Plot the point.

**4.** Plot the point for each number pair, in order. Then use a straightedge to connect the points in the order you plotted them. Can you solve the riddle?

X ⟶                                     Y ↑

| | | |
|---|---|---|
| 6 x 5 = 30 | 11 x 5 = 55 | (Example) |
| 7 x 5 = _____ | 5 x 7 = _____ | |
| 5 x 11 = _____ | 7 x 5 = _____ | |
| 5 x 8 = _____ | 5 x 5 = _____ | |
| 5 x 9 = _____ | 5 x 1 = _____ | |
| 5 x 6 = _____ | 5 x 4 = _____ | |
| 3 x 5 = _____ | 1 x 5 = _____ | |
| 4 x 5 = _____ | 5 x 5 = _____ | |
| 5 x 1 = _____ | 5 x 7 = _____ | |
| 5 x 5 = _____ | 7 x 5 = _____ | |
| 5 x 6 = _____ | 11 x 5 = _____ | |

## EXTRA CHALLENGE!

Arnold has a pocketful of nickels and dimes that equal one dollar. He has half as many dimes as nickels. How many nickels does he have?_____

Great Graph Art: Multiplication & Division Scholastic Professional Books

Name_____

# COYOTE BY MOONLIGHT

**What has hands and gets into stick-ups with cowboys?**_____

To find out the answer, solve the problems on page 16. Then plot the number pairs and connect the points. The picture you make will help you solve the riddle. (The answer is upside down at the bottom of this page.)

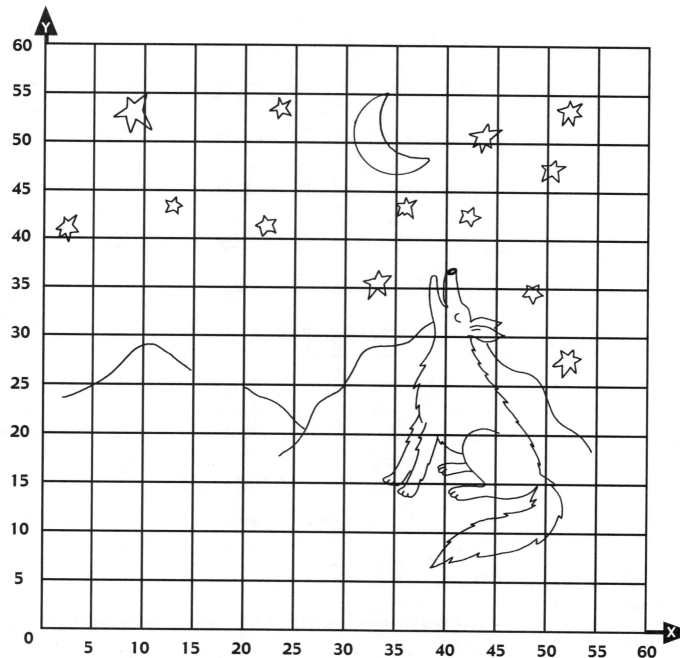

Great Graph Art: Multiplication & Division Scholastic Professional Books

**Name**_____

# COYOTE BY MOONLIGHT

**1.** Solve each multiplication problem. Example problems have been done for you.

**2.** In the example problems, the numbers **20** and **10** are called a number pair. We write (20, 10).

**3.** Look at the graph on page 15. Graph the number pairs in the example. Start at 0.
Go across to the number **20** and up to the number **10**. Plot the point.

**4.** Plot the point for each number pair. Then use a straightedge to connect the points in the order you plotted them. Can you solve the riddle?

X ⟶　　　　　　　　　　　　Y ↑

| | |
|---|---|
| 4　x　5　=　20 | 2　x　5　=　10　(Example) |
| 5　x　4　=　_____ | 5　x　5　=　_____ |
| 6　x　5　=　_____ | 5　x　6　=　_____ |
| 5　x　6　=　_____ | 10　x　5　=　_____ |
| 5　x　5　=　_____ | 5　x　10　=　_____ |
| 5　x　5　=　_____ | 7　x　5　=　_____ |
| 4　x　5　=　_____ | 5　x　7　=　_____ |
| 5　x　4　=　_____ | 11　x　5　=　_____ |
| 5　x　3　=　_____ | 5　x　11　=　_____ |
| 3　x　5　=　_____ | 8　x　5　=　_____ |
| 2　x　5　=　_____ | 5　x　8　=　_____ |
| 5　x　2　=　_____ | 5　x　10　=　_____ |
| 1　x　5　=　_____ | 10　x　5　=　_____ |
| 5　x　1　=　_____ | 7　x　5　=　_____ |
| 5　x　3　=　_____ | 6　x　5　=　_____ |
| 3　x　5　=　_____ | 2　x　5　=　_____ |
| 4　x　5　=　_____ | 5　x　2　=　_____ |

## EXTRA CHALLENGE!

Why did the cowboy get a job as a comedian?
Shade the boxes that contain numbers that are multiples of 5. The letters in the unshaded boxes spell the answer to the riddle. (Read from left to right.)

| H | 12 | E | 7 | R | 15 | W | 11 | O | 25 | A | 16 | S | 18 | A | 6 | L | 26 | W | 52 |
|---|---|---|---|---|---|---|---|---|---|---|---|---|---|---|---|---|---|---|---|
| T | 35 | A | 14 | Y | 17 | S | 13 | H | 19 | O | 36 | P | 45 | R | 37 | S | 46 | I | 48 |
| N | 4 | G | 12 | A | 23 | T | 10 | R | 42 | O | 41 | U | 19 | B | 30 | N | 6 | D | 63 |

*Great Graph Art: Multiplication & Division Scholastic Professional Books*

# THE MERMAID TEACHER

**Why did the mermaid give up her teaching job?** _____

To find out the answer, solve the problems on page 18. Then plot the number pairs and connect the points. The picture you make will help you solve the riddle. (The answer is upside down at the bottom of this page.)

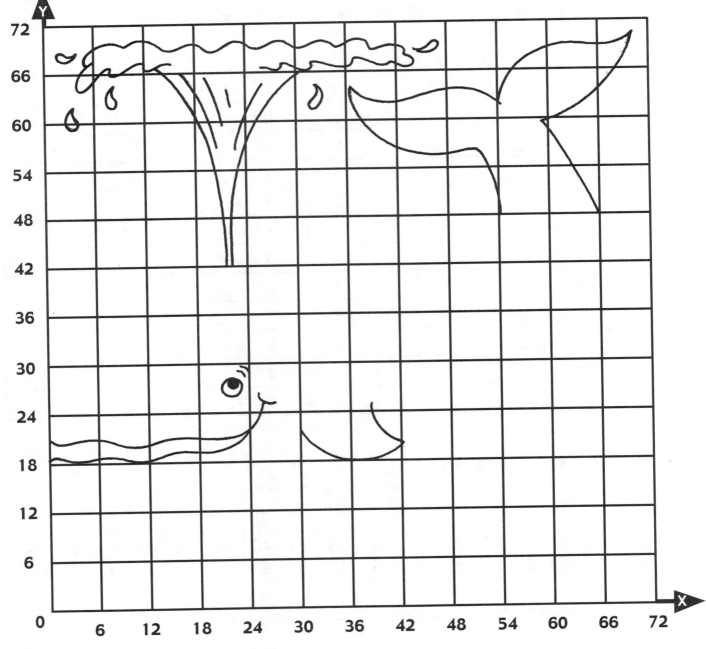

Answer: *She was tired of the whales spouting off!*

# THE MERMAID TEACHER

**1.** Solve each multiplication problem. Example problems have been done for you.

**2.** In the example problems, the numbers **0** and **18** are called a number pair. We write (0, 18).

**3.** Look at the graph on page 17. Graph the number pairs in the example. Start at 0. Stay at the number **0** and go up to the number **18**. Plot the point.

**4.** Plot the point for each number pair, in order. Then use a straightedge to connect the points in the order you plotted them. After the word STOP, start a new line. Can you solve the riddle?

| | | |
|---|---|---|
| **X** → | **Y** ↑ | |
| 6 x 0 = 0 | 6 x 3 = 18 | (Example) |
| 6 x 1 = ____ | 2 x 6 = ____ | |
| 6 x 7 = ____ | 6 x 2 = ____ | |
| 9 x 6 = ____ | 6 x 3 = ____ | |
| 6 x 11 = ____ | 6 x 5 = ____ | |
| 11 x 6 = ____ | 6 x 8 = ____ | STOP |
| 9 x 6 = ____ | 8 x 6 = ____ | |
| 6 x 9 = ____ | 7 x 6 = ____ | |
| 4 x 6 = ____ | 6 x 7 = ____ | |
| 6 x 1 = ____ | 7 x 6 = ____ | |
| 0 x 6 = ____ | 6 x 6 = ____ | |
| 6 x 0 = ____ | 6 x 3 = ____ | |

## EXTRA CHALLENGE!

Do you know why the mermaid wrote a novel? To find out, shade every block that is a multiple of 6. The corresponding letters will spell out the answer.

| 5 | 6 | 12 | 18 | 19 | 22 | 24 | 30 | 35 | 36 | 40 | 41 | 42 | 47 | 48 | 51 | 54 |
|---|---|---|---|---|---|---|---|---|---|---|---|---|---|---|---|---|
| R | A | L | O | X | M | N | G | K | T | B | J | A | P | L | Q | E |

Write the answer here. She had _____.

# A TRIP TO THE DENTIST

**Why did the king go to the dentist ?** _____

To find out the answer, solve the problems on page 20. Then plot the number pairs and connect the points. The picture you make will help you solve the riddle. (The answer is upside down at the bottom of this page.)

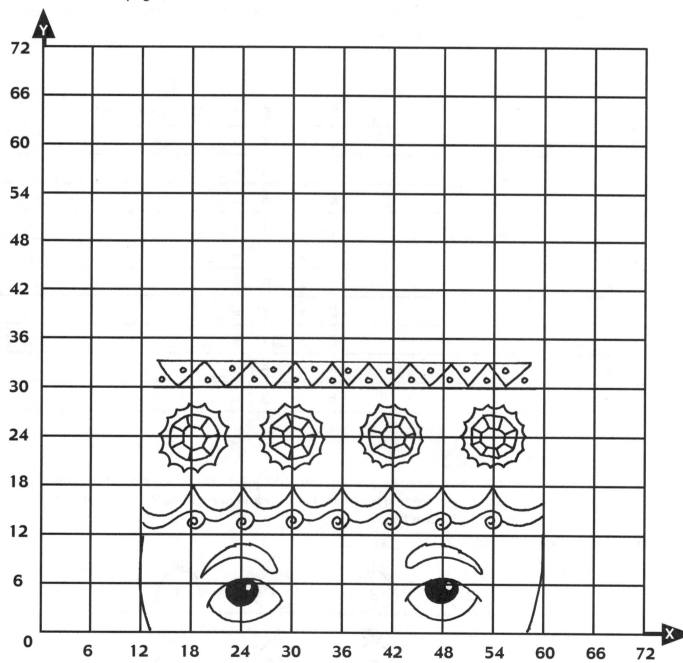

Answer: **for a crown**

# A TRIP TO THE DENTIST

**1.** Solve each multiplication problem. Example problems have been done for you.

**2.** In the example problems, the numbers **60** and **12** are called a number pair. We write (60, 12).

**3.** Look at the graph on page 19. Graph the number pairs in the example. Start at 0.
Go across to the number **60** and up to the number **12**. Plot the point.

**4.** Plot the point for each number pair, in order. Then use a straightedge to connect the points in the order you plotted them. Can you solve the riddle?

X ⟶          Y ↑

| | | | |
|---|---|---|---|
| 10 x 6 = 60 | | 2 x 6 = 12 (Example) | |
| 6 x 10 = _____ | | 6 x 4 = _____ | |
| 9 x 6 = _____ | | 11 x 6 = _____ | |
| 6 x 8 = _____ | | 6 x 6 = _____ | |
| 6 x 7 = _____ | | 6 x 11 = _____ | |
| 6 x 6 = _____ | | 6 x 6 = _____ | |
| 5 x 6 = _____ | | 11 x 6 = _____ | |
| 4 x 6 = _____ | | 6 x 6 = _____ | |
| 6 x 3 = _____ | | 6 x 11 = _____ | |
| 6 x 2 = _____ | | 4 x 6 = _____ | |
| 2 x 6 = _____ | | 6 x 2 = _____ | |

## EXTRA CHALLENGE!

The Tooth Fairy is making a crown with shiny white teeth. She needs 72 more teeth to finish the crown. Look at the number on each bag of teeth in the Tooth Fairy's warehouse. Multiply the number by 6 to find out how many teeth are in each bag.

Which bag will have 72 teeth in it?_____

*Great Graph Art: Multiplication & Division Scholastic Professional Books*

# UP, UP, AND AWAY

**I like to fly in the bright blue sky, soaring ever higher—until I meet a wire!**
**What am I?** _____

To find out the answer, solve the problems on page 22. Then plot the number pairs and connect the points. The picture you make will help you solve the riddle. (The answer is upside down at the bottom of this page.)

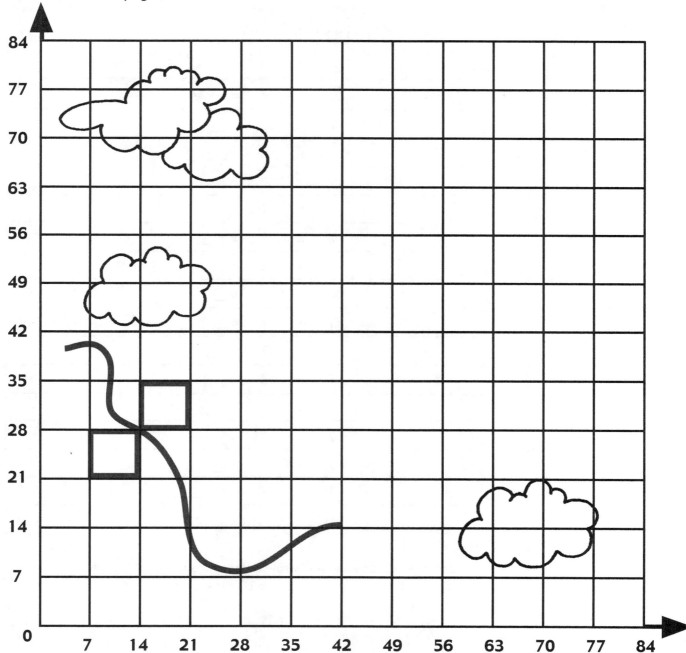

Name_____

# UP, UP, AND AWAY

**1.** Solve each multiplication problem. Example problems have been done for you.

**2.** In the example problems, the numbers **42** and **14** are called a number pair. We write (42, 14).

**3.** Look at the graph on page 21. Graph the number pairs in the example. Start at 0.
Go across to the number **42** and up to the number **14**. Plot the point.

**4.** Plot the point for each number pair, in order. Then use a straightedge to connect the points in the order you plotted them. After the word STOP, start a new line. Can you solve the riddle?

| X → | Y ↑ |
|---|---|
| 6 x 7 = 42 | 2 x 7 = 14 (Example) |
| 7 x 11 = _____ | 7 x 7 = _____ |
| 7 x 10 = _____ | 7 x 9 = _____ |
| 9 x 7 = _____ | 11 x 7 = _____ |
| 7 x 7 = _____ | 10 x 7 = _____ |
| 5 x 7 = _____ | 7 x 9 = _____ |
| 7 x 6 = _____ | 7 x 2 = _____ STOP |
| 7 x 2 = _____ | 7 x 1 = _____ |
| 3 x 7 = _____ | 1 x 7 = _____ |
| 7 x 3 = _____ | 3 x 7 = _____ |
| 7 x 4 = _____ | 7 x 3 = _____ |
| 4 x 7 = _____ | 7 x 2 = _____ |
| 3 x 7 = _____ | 2 x 7 = _____ |
| 7 x 2 = _____ | 7 x 2 = _____ |
| 2 x 7 = _____ | 1 x 7 = _____ |

# EXTRA CHALLENGE!

Which kite belongs to Pauley? Read the clues below and draw a circle around Pauley's kite. The number on Pauley's kite is a multiple of 7. It is greater than 7 x 3.  It is less than 7 x 6.

*Great Graph Art: Multiplication & Division Scholastic Professional Books*

# MATH TEST

**Why did the student eat his math test?** _____

To find out the answer, solve the problems on page 24. Then plot the number pairs and connect the points. The picture you make will help you solve the riddle. (The answer is upside down at the bottom of this page.)

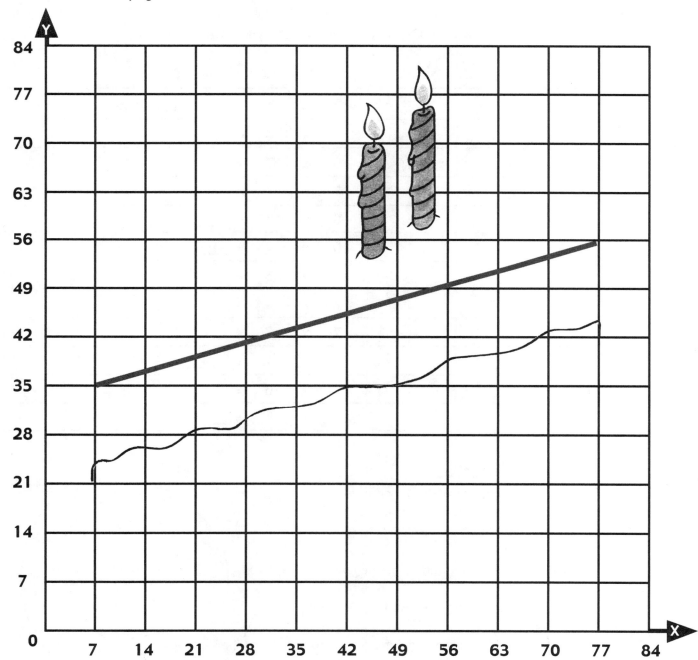

# MATH TEST

**1.** Solve each multiplication problem. Example problems have been done for you.

**2.** In the example problems, the numbers **7** and **7** are called a number pair. We write (7, 7).

**3.** Look at the graph on page 23. Graph the number pair in the example. Start at 0.
Go across to the number **7** and up to the number **7**. Plot the point.

**4.** Plot the point for each number pair, in order. Then use a straightedge to connect the points in the order you plotted them. After the word STOP, start a new line. Can you solve the riddle?

| X ⟶ | | | Y ↑ | | |
|---|---|---|---|---|---|
| **1 x 7 = 7** | | | **7 x 1 = 7** | | **(Example)** |
| 7 x 11 = _____ | | | 7 x 4 = _____ | | |
| 11 x 7 = _____ | | | 5 x 7 = _____ | | |
| 7 x 11 = _____ | | | 7 x 7 = _____ | | |
| 11 x 7 = _____ | | | 8 x 7 = _____ | | |
| 7 x 8 = _____ | | | 10 x 7 = _____ | | |
| 1 x 7 = _____ | | | 7 x 5 = _____ | | |
| 7 x 1 = _____ | | | 7 x 4 = _____ | | |
| 1 x 7 = _____ | | | 7 x 2 = _____ | | |
| 7 x 1 = _____ | | | 7 x 1 = _____ STOP | | |
| 7 x 11 = _____ | | | 7 x 6 = _____ | | |
| 1 x 7 = _____ | | | 3 x 7 = _____ | | |

## EXTRA CHALLENGE!

Sue and Tony are playing a game of "product darts."
Each player throws two darts. Then they multiply the two
numbers together to get their scores. Answer these
questions about their games:

**a.** If Tony's score is 21, what two numbers did he land on?
_____  _____

**b.** If Sue's score is 81, what two numbers did she land on?
_____  _____

**c.** If Tony's score is 21, and Sue's score is 7 more than Tony's,
what numbers did Sue land on?

_____  _____

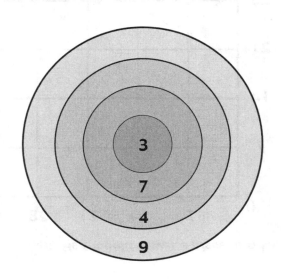

Name_____

# LETTERS AND FLOWERS

**What do flowers and the letter "A" have in common ?** _____

To find out the answer, solve the problems on page 26. Then plot the number pairs and connect the points. The picture you make will help you solve the riddle. (The answer is upside down at the bottom of this page.)

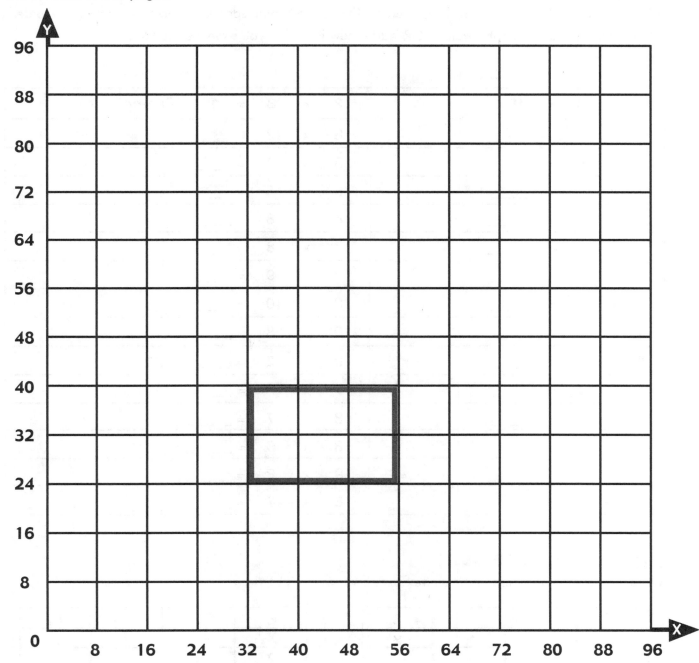

Answer: *A bee (B) comes after both of them.*

25

# LETTERS AND FLOWERS

**1.** Solve each multiplication problem. Example problems have been done for you.

**2.** In the example problems, the numbers **16** and **16** are called a number pair. We write (16, 16).

**3.** Look at the graph on page 25. Graph the number pair in the example. Start at 0.
Go across to the number **16** and up to the number **16**. Plot the point.

**4.** Plot the point for each number pair, in order. Then use a straightedge to connect the points in the order you plotted them. After the word STOP, start a new line. Can you solve the riddle?

X ➡                                      Y ⬆

| | | | | |
|---|---|---|---|---|
| 2 x 8 = 16 | | 2 x 8 = 16 (Example) | | |
| 8 x 8 = _____ | | 8 x 2 = _____ | | |
| 9 x 8 = _____ | | 8 x 3 = _____ | | |
| 8 x 9 = _____ | | 8 x 5 = _____ | | |
| 8 x 8 = _____ | | 6 x 8 = _____ | | |
| 8 x 9 = _____ | | 7 x 8 = _____ | | |
| 9 x 8 = _____ | | 8 x 9 = _____ | | |
| 8 x 8 = _____ | | 8 x 10 = _____ | | |
| 2 x 8 = _____ | | 10 x 8 = _____ | | |
| 8 x 2 = _____ | | 8 x 2 = _____ STOP | | |
| 4 x 8 = _____ | | 7 x 8 = _____ | | |
| 7 x 8 = _____ | | 8 x 7 = _____ | | |
| 8 x 7 = _____ | | 8 x 9 = _____ | | |
| 8 x 4 = _____ | | 9 x 8 = _____ | | |
| 4 x 8 = _____ | | 8 x 7 = _____ | | |

## EXTRA CHALLENGE!

Write the missing numbers in the white boxes below.

| | | | |
|---|---|---|---|
| 8 | x | | 8 |
| x | | x | x |
| 1 | x | | |
| | x | | 32 |

| | | | |
|---|---|---|---|
| 6 | x | | 12 |
| x | | x | x |
| 2 | x | | |
| | x | | 96 |

Great Graph Art: Multiplication & Division Scholastic Professional Books

Name_____

# HOME SWEET HOME

**What kind of house doesn't weigh very much?** _____

To find out the answer, solve the problems on page 28. Then plot the number pairs and connect the points. The picture you make will help you solve the riddle. (The answer is upside down at the bottom of this page.)

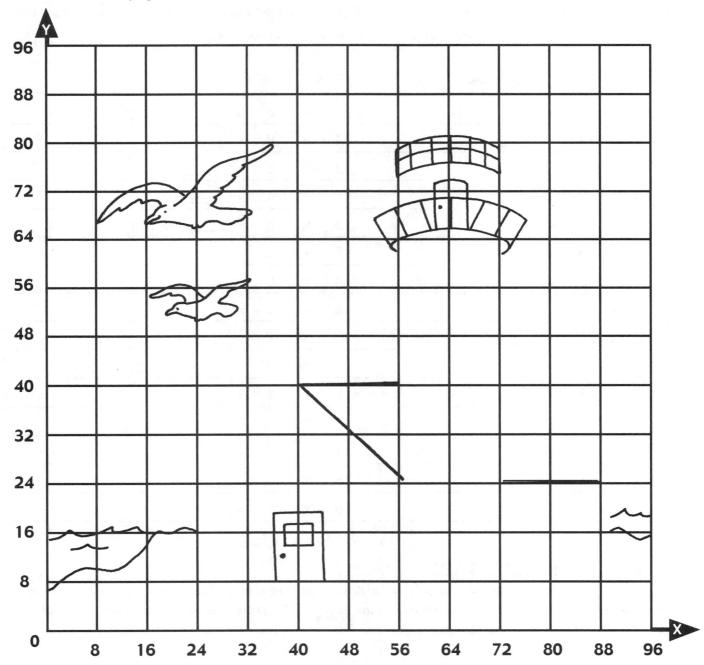

Answer: a lighthouse

# HOME SWEET HOME

**1.** Solve each multiplication problem. Example problems have been done for you.

**2.** In the example problems, the numbers **24** and **8** are called a number pair. We write (24, 8).

**3.** Look at the graph on page 27. Graph the number pair in the example. Start at 0.
Go across to the number **24** and up to the number **8**. Plot the point.

**4.** Plot the point for each number pair, in order. Then use a straightedge to connect the points in the order you plotted them. After the word STOP, start a new line. Can you solve the riddle?

| X ⟶ | Y ↑ |
|---|---|
| **3 x 8 = 24** | **1 x 8 = 8 (Example)** |
| 8 x 11 = _____ | 1 x 8 = _____ |
| 11 x 8 = _____ | 3 x 8 = _____ |
| 10 x 8 = _____ | 8 x 4 = _____ |
| 8 x 9 = _____ | 8 x 5 = _____ STOP |
| 8 x 5 = _____ | 5 x 8 = _____ |
| 4 x 8 = _____ | 4 x 8 = _____ |
| 8 x 3 = _____ | 8 x 3 = _____ |
| 3 x 8 = _____ | 8 x 2 = _____ |
| 8 x 3 = _____ | 1 x 8 = _____ STOP |
| 8 x 7 = _____ | 8 x 1 = _____ |
| 7 x 8 = _____ | 10 x 8 = _____ |
| 8 x 8 = _____ | 11 x 8 = _____ |
| 9 x 8 = _____ | 8 x 10 = _____ |
| 8 x 9 = _____ | 8 x 1 = _____ |

## EXTRA CHALLENGE!

Many people know that spiders have eight legs. But did you know that most spiders have eight eyes, too? If there are five spiders on a web and they all look at you at the same time, how many spider eyes are staring at you?_____

# BOAT SHOPPING

**What is the cheapest kind of boat to buy?** _____

To find out the answer, solve the problems on page 30. Then plot the number pairs and connect the points. The picture you make will help you solve the riddle. (The answer is upside down at the bottom of this page.)

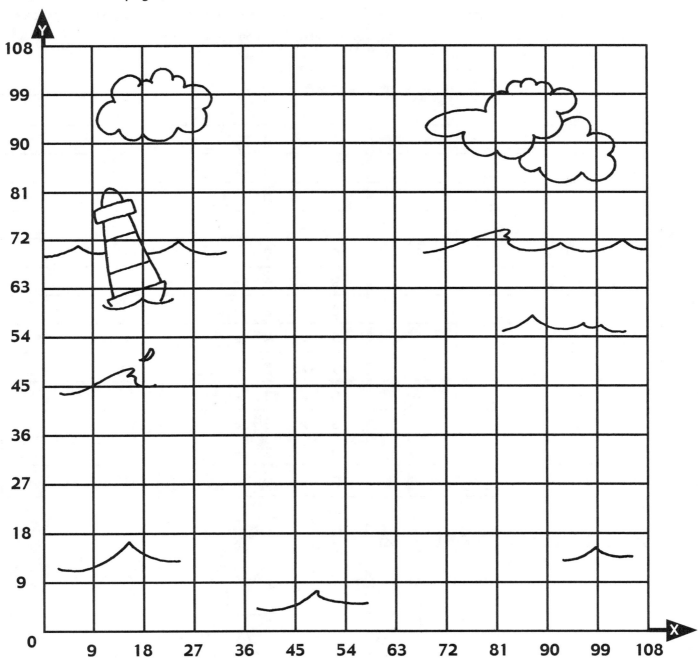

**Name**_____

# BOAT SHOPPING

**1.** Solve each multiplication problem. Example problems have been done for you.

**2.** In the example problems, the numbers **27** and **9** are called a number pair. We write (27, 9).

**3.** Look at the graph on page 29. Graph the number pair in the example. Start at 0.
Go across to the number **27** and up to the number **9**. Plot the point.

**4.** Plot the point for each number pair, in order. Then use a straightedge to connect the points in the order
you plotted them. After the word STOP, start a new line. Can you solve the riddle?

X ⟶ Y ↑

| | | | | | | | | |
|---|---|---|---|---|---|---|---|---|
| 9 | x | 3 | = | 27 | 9 | x | 1 | = | 9 (Example) |
| 9 | x | 4 | = _____ | 1 | x | 9 | = _____ |
| 9 | x | 9 | = _____ | 9 | x | 1 | = _____ |
| 10 | x | 9 | = _____ | 1 | x | 9 | = _____ |
| 9 | x | 11 | = _____ | 9 | x | 3 | = _____ |
| 9 | x | 8 | = _____ | 9 | x | 7 | = _____ |
| 5 | x | 9 | = _____ | 9 | x | 11 | = _____ |
| 9 | x | 3 | = _____ | 6 | x | 9 | = _____ |
| 9 | x | 2 | = _____ | 3 | x | 9 | = _____ |
| 3 | x | 9 | = _____ | 1 | x | 9 | = _____ STOP |
| 9 | x | 5 | = _____ | 9 | x | 11 | = _____ |
| 5 | x | 9 | = _____ | 3 | x | 9 | = _____ STOP |
| 2 | x | 9 | = _____ | 9 | x | 3 | = _____ |
| 9 | x | 11 | = _____ | 3 | x | 9 | = _____ |

## EXTRA CHALLENGE!
Multiply to complete the circle.

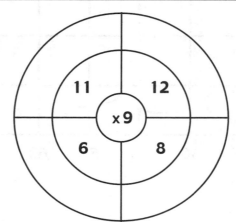

Great Graph Art: Multiplication & Division Scholastic Professional Books

# LOCKED COFFIN

**What do you use to open a locked coffin?** _____

To find out the answer, solve the problems on page 32. Then plot the number pairs and connect the points. The picture you make will help you solve the riddle. (The answer is upside down at the bottom of this page.)

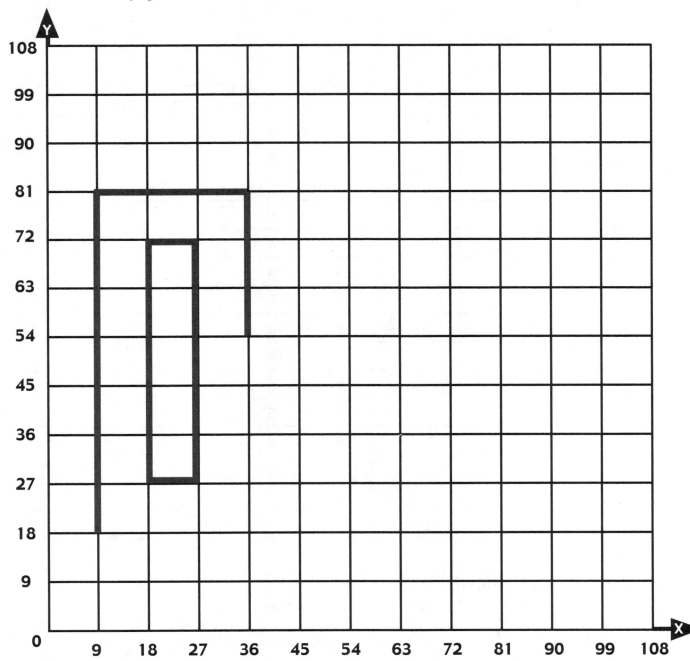

Answer: a skeleton key

# LOCKED COFFIN

**1.** Solve each multiplication problem. Example problems have been done for you.

**2.** In the example problems, the numbers **9** and **18** are called a number pair. We write (9,18).

**3.** Look at the graph on page 31. Graph the number pair in the example. Start at 0.
Go across to the number **9** and up to the number **18**. Plot the point.

**4.** Plot the point for each number pair, in order. Then use a straightedge to connect the points in the order you plotted them. Can you solve the riddle?

X $\longrightarrow$        Y $\uparrow$

| | | |
|---|---|---|
| 9 x 1 = 9 | 9 x 2 = 18 (Example) |
| 9 x 4 = _____ | 9 x 2 = _____ |
| 4 x 9 = _____ | 9 x 5 = _____ |
| 9 x 7 = _____ | 5 x 9 = _____ |
| 7 x 9 = _____ | 4 x 9 = _____ |
| 8 x 9 = _____ | 9 x 4 = _____ |
| 9 x 8 = _____ | 9 x 5 = _____ |
| 9 x 9 = _____ | 5 x 9 = _____ |
| 9 x 9 = _____ | 9 x 3 = _____ |
| 9 x 10 = _____ | 3 x 9 = _____ |
| 10 x 9 = _____ | 9 x 5 = _____ |
| 9 x 11 = _____ | 5 x 9 = _____ |
| 11 x 9 = _____ | 9 x 4 = _____ |
| 9 x 12 = _____ | 4 x 9 = _____ |
| 12 x 9 = _____ | 6 x 9 = _____ |
| 9 x 4 = _____ | 9 x 6 = _____ |

## EXTRA CHALLENGE!

Place the numbers 1 to 9 inside the boxes in the problems below. Use each number only once.

$$\begin{array}{r} 9 \\ \times\ 4 \\ \hline \square\square \end{array} \qquad \begin{array}{r} 9 \\ \times\ \square \\ \hline 18 \end{array} \qquad \begin{array}{r} 9 \\ \times\ 6 \\ \hline \square\square \end{array} \qquad \begin{array}{r} 9 \\ \times\ \square \\ \hline 63 \end{array} \qquad \begin{array}{r} 9 \\ \times\ 9 \\ \hline \square\square \end{array} \qquad \begin{array}{r} \square \\ \times\ 2 \\ \hline 18 \end{array}$$

*Great Graph Art: Multiplication & Division Scholastic Professional Books*

Name _____

# TOUCHDOWN

**I like to make touchdowns, but I never wear shoulder pads. What am I?** _____

To find out the answer, solve the problems on page 34. Then plot the number pairs and connect the points. The picture you make will help you solve the riddle. (The answer is upside down at the bottom of this page.)

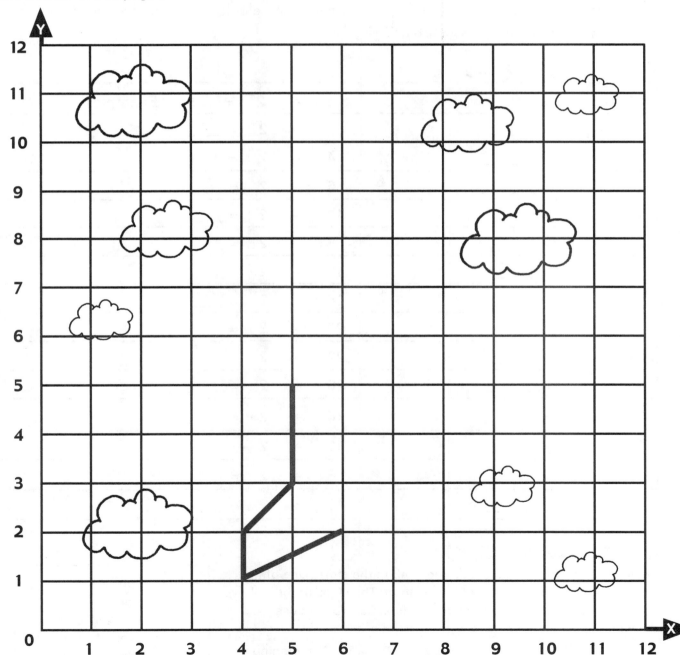

Answer: an airplane

# TOUCHDOWN

**1.** Solve each division problem. Example problems have been done for you.

**2.** In the example problems, the numbers **6** and **2** are called a number pair. We write (6, 2).

**3.** Look at the graph on page 33. Graph the number pair in the example. Start at 0. Go across to the number **6** and up to the number **2**. Plot the point.

**4.** Plot the point for each number pair, in order. Then use a straightedge to connect the points in the order you plotted them. Can you solve the riddle?

| X ⟶ | | Y ↑ | |
|---|---|---|---|
| 12 ÷ 2 = 6 | | 4 ÷ 2 = 2 (Example) | |
| 16 ÷ 2 = _____ | | 2 ÷ 2 = _____ | |
| 16 ÷ 2 = _____ | | 4 ÷ 2 = _____ | |
| 14 ÷ 2 = _____ | | 6 ÷ 2 = _____ | |
| 14 ÷ 2 = _____ | | 10 ÷ 2 = _____ | |
| 22 ÷ 2 = _____ | | 8 ÷ 2 = _____ | |
| 14 ÷ 2 = _____ | | 16 ÷ 2 = _____ | |
| 14 ÷ 2 = _____ | | 18 ÷ 2 = _____ | |
| 14 ÷ 2 = _____ | | 20 ÷ 2 = _____ | |
| 12 ÷ 2 = _____ | | 22 ÷ 2 = _____ | |
| 10 ÷ 2 = _____ | | 20 ÷ 2 = _____ | |
| 10 ÷ 2 = _____ | | 18 ÷ 2 = _____ | |
| 10 ÷ 2 = _____ | | 16 ÷ 2 = _____ | |
| 2 ÷ 2 = _____ | | 8 ÷ 2 = _____ | |
| 10 ÷ 2 = _____ | | 10 ÷ 2 = _____ | |

## EXTRA CHALLENGE!

There are five boxes of cereal on the shelf in the store. One of the boxes has a coupon in it for a free vacation. The clues (right) tell about the number code on the winning box. Can you choose the winning cereal box?

| 126 | 145 | 168 | 148 | 100 |

The winning cereal box is _____.

- I have three digits.
- My first digit is 1.
- When you divide my second digit by 2, you get the answer 2.
- When you divide my third digit by 4, you get the answer 2.

*Great Graph Art: Multiplication & Division Scholastic Professional Books*

# FLYING BUTTER

**Why did the little boy throw butter out the window?**_____

To find out the answer, solve the problems on page 36. Then plot the number pairs and connect the points. The picture you make will help you solve the riddle. (The answer is upside down at the bottom of this page.)

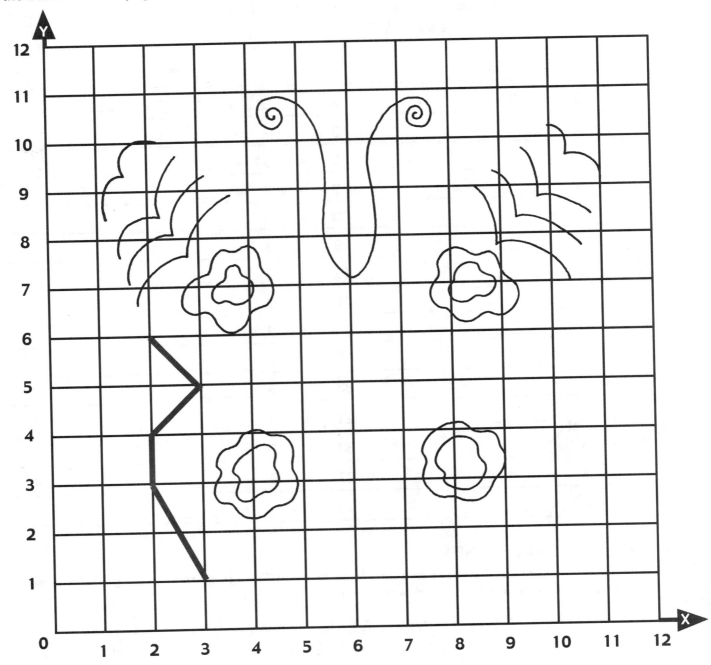

Answer: **He wanted to see butterfly.**

Name_____

# FLYING BUTTER

**1.** Solve each division problem. Example problems have been done for you.

**2.** In the example problems, the numbers **3** and **1** are called a number pair. We write (3,1).

**3.** Look at the graph on page 35. Graph the number pair in the example. Start at 0.
Go across to the number **3** and up to the number **1**. Plot the point.

**4.** Plot the point for each number pair, in order. Then use a straightedge to connect the points in the order you plotted them. Can you solve the riddle?

| X ⟶ | Y ↑ |
|---|---|
| **9** ÷ **3** = **3** | **3** ÷ **3** = **1** (Example) |
| 12 ÷ 3 = _____ | 3 ÷ 3 = _____ |
| 18 ÷ 3 = _____ | 9 ÷ 3 = _____ |
| 24 ÷ 3 = _____ | 3 ÷ 3 = _____ |
| 27 ÷ 3 = _____ | 3 ÷ 3 = _____ |
| 30 ÷ 3 = _____ | 9 ÷ 3 = _____ |
| 30 ÷ 3 = _____ | 12 ÷ 3 = _____ |
| 27 ÷ 3 = _____ | 15 ÷ 3 = _____ |
| 30 ÷ 3 = _____ | 18 ÷ 3 = _____ |
| 33 ÷ 3 = _____ | 27 ÷ 3 = _____ |
| 33 ÷ 3 = _____ | 33 ÷ 3 = _____ |
| 18 ÷ 3 = _____ | 21 ÷ 3 = _____ |
| 3 ÷ 3 = _____ | 33 ÷ 3 = _____ |
| 3 ÷ 3 = _____ | 27 ÷ 3 = _____ |
| 6 ÷ 3 = _____ | 18 ÷ 3 = _____ |

## EXTRA CHALLENGE!

Lasso Larry is rounding up three cows at a time to be branded. Put a ring around each group of three.
How many groups of cows will Lasso Larry take in all? _____

*Great Graph Art: Multiplication & Division Scholastic Professional Books*

# RING! RING!

**I demand that you answer me fast, but I never ask questions. What am I?**_____

To find out the answer, solve the problems on page 38. Then plot the number pairs and connect the points. The picture you make will help you solve the riddle. (The answer is upside down at the bottom of this page.)

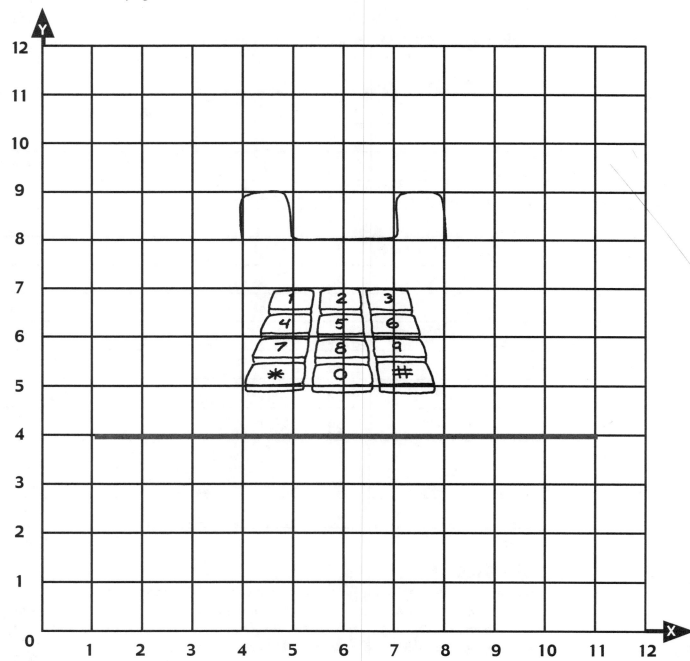

Answer: a telephone

**Name**_____

# RING! RING!

**1.** Solve each division problem. Example problems have been done for you.

**2.** In the example problems, the numbers **1** and **4** are called a number pair. We write (1, 4).

**3.** Look at the graph on page 37. Graph the number pairs in the example. Start at 0.
Go across to the number **1** and up to the number **4**. Plot the point.

**4.** Plot the point for each number pair, in order. Then use a straightedge to connect the points in the order you plotted them. After the word STOP, start a new line. Can you solve the riddle?

| X → | Y ↑ |
|---|---|
| 4 ÷ 4 = 1 | 16 ÷ 4 = 4 (Example) |
| 4 ÷ 4 = _____ | 8 ÷ 4 = _____ |
| 44 ÷ 4 = _____ | 8 ÷ 4 = _____ |
| 44 ÷ 4 = _____ | 16 ÷ 4 = _____ |
| 32 ÷ 4 = _____ | 32 ÷ 4 = _____ STOP |
| 36 ÷ 4 = _____ | 28 ÷ 4 = _____ |
| 44 ÷ 4 = _____ | 28 ÷ 4 = _____ |
| 44 ÷ 4 = _____ | 32 ÷ 4 = _____ |
| 40 ÷ 4 = _____ | 40 ÷ 4 = _____ |
| 8 ÷ 4 = _____ | 40 ÷ 4 = _____ |
| 4 ÷ 4 = _____ | 32 ÷ 4 = _____ |
| 4 ÷ 4 = _____ | 28 ÷ 4 = _____ |
| 12 ÷ 4 = _____ | 28 ÷ 4 = _____ STOP |
| 16 ÷ 4 = _____ | 32 ÷ 4 = _____ |
| 4 ÷ 4 = _____ | 16 ÷ 4 = _____ |

## EXTRA CHALLENGE!

Tom's mom is a math professor, and she is always trying to get Tom to think about math. She covered the numbers on the telephone with stickers and changed the numbers to multiples of four. For example, she changed the 1 to a 4, because 1 x 4 = 4. She changed the 2 to an 8, because 2 x 4 = 8 and so on. When Tom called his best friend he dialed:   **8 36 28– 12 8 24 0**

What is Tom's friend's real phone number?_____

*Great Graph Art: Multiplication & Division Scholastic Professional Books*

Name_____

# BIRD OF PEACE

**What happened when the bird of peace dropped his olive branch?** _____

To find out the answer, solve the problems on page 40. Then plot the number pairs and connect the points. The picture you make will help you solve the riddle. (The answer is upside down at the bottom of this page.)

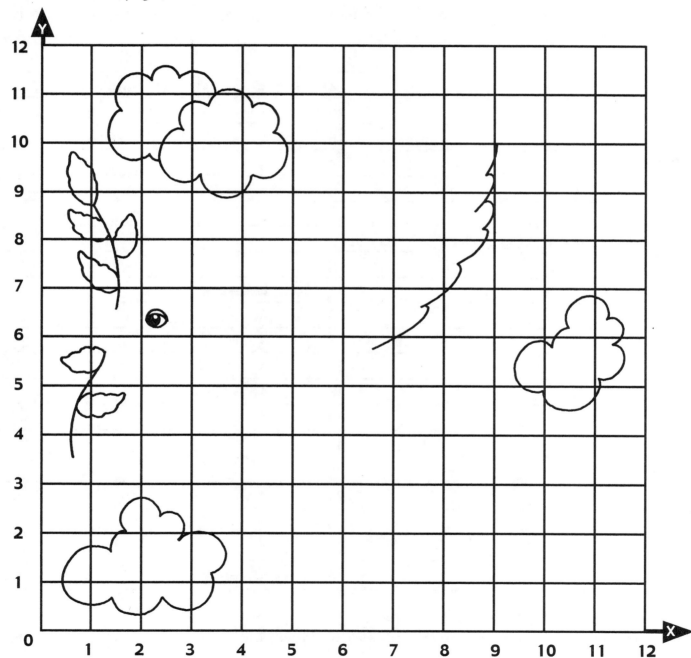

Answer: *He dove for it.*

**Name**_____

# BIRD OF PEACE

**1.** Solve each division problem. Example problems have been done for you.

**2.** In the example problems, the numbers **1** and **6** are called a number pair. We write (1, 6).

**3.** Look at the graph on page 39. Graph the number pair in the example. Start at 0. Go across to the number **1** and up to the number **6**. Plot the point.

**4.** Plot the point for each number pair, in order. Then use a straightedge to connect the points in the order you plotted them. Can you solve the riddle?

**X ⟶**  **Y ↑**

| | | | | | | | | | |
|---|---|---|---|---|---|---|---|---|---|
| 4 | ÷ | 4 | = | 1 | 24 | ÷ | 4 | = | 6 (Example) |
| 8 | ÷ | 4 | = _____ | | 20 | ÷ | 4 | = _____ | |
| 8 | ÷ | 4 | = _____ | | 16 | ÷ | 4 | = _____ | |
| 16 | ÷ | 4 | = _____ | | 8 | ÷ | 4 | = _____ | |
| 24 | ÷ | 4 | = _____ | | 8 | ÷ | 4 | = _____ | |
| 28 | ÷ | 4 | = _____ | | 12 | ÷ | 4 | = _____ | |
| 32 | ÷ | 4 | = _____ | | 8 | ÷ | 4 | = _____ | |
| 44 | ÷ | 4 | = _____ | | 8 | ÷ | 4 | = _____ | |
| 44 | ÷ | 4 | = _____ | | 12 | ÷ | 4 | = _____ | |
| 32 | ÷ | 4 | = _____ | | 20 | ÷ | 4 | = _____ | |
| 40 | ÷ | 4 | = _____ | | 28 | ÷ | 4 | = _____ | |
| 44 | ÷ | 4 | = _____ | | 36 | ÷ | 4 | = _____ | |
| 44 | ÷ | 4 | = _____ | | 48 | ÷ | 4 | = _____ | |
| 36 | ÷ | 4 | = _____ | | 40 | ÷ | 4 | = _____ | |
| 36 | ÷ | 4 | = _____ | | 48 | ÷ | 4 | = _____ | |
| 16 | ÷ | 4 | = _____ | | 28 | ÷ | 4 | = _____ | |
| 16 | ÷ | 4 | = _____ | | 24 | ÷ | 4 | = _____ | |
| 12 | ÷ | 4 | = _____ | | 28 | ÷ | 4 | = _____ | |
| 8 | ÷ | 4 | = _____ | | 28 | ÷ | 4 | = _____ | |
| 4 | ÷ | 4 | = _____ | | 24 | ÷ | 4 | = _____ | |

## EXTRA CHALLENGE!

Mia's phone number is written in secret code. Help her friend Sasha figure out her real phone number by dividing each number by 4.

32  16  36  -  8  12  20  4

Write your phone number using the secret code. _____

*Great Graph Art: Multiplication & Division Scholastic Professional Books*

# KING JOHN

**How did people know that King John would never give up his reign?** _____

_____

To find out the answer, solve the problems on page 42. Then plot the number pairs and connect the points. The picture you make will help you solve the riddle. (The answer is upside down at the bottom of this page.)

# KING JOHN

**1.** Solve each division problem. Example problems have been done for you.

**2.** In the example problems, the numbers **6** and **1** are called a number pair. We write (6,1).

**3.** Look at the graph on page 41. Graph the number pair in the example. Start at 0. Go across to the number **6** and up to the number **1**. Plot the point.

**4.** Plot the point for each number pair, in order. Then use a straightedge to connect the points in the order you plotted them. Can you solve the riddle?

X ⟶                                                          Y ⬆

| | | | | | | | | | |
|---|---|---|---|---|---|---|---|---|---|
| 30 | ÷ | 5 | = | 6 | 5 | ÷ | 5 | = | 1 (Example) |
| 30 | ÷ | 5 | = _____ | | 30 | ÷ | 5 | = _____ | |
| 35 | ÷ | 5 | = _____ | | 35 | ÷ | 5 | = _____ | |
| 40 | ÷ | 5 | = _____ | | 30 | ÷ | 5 | = _____ | |
| 45 | ÷ | 5 | = _____ | | 35 | ÷ | 5 | = _____ | |
| 50 | ÷ | 5 | = _____ | | 30 | ÷ | 5 | = _____ | |
| 55 | ÷ | 5 | = _____ | | 35 | ÷ | 5 | = _____ | |
| 30 | ÷ | 5 | = _____ | | 55 | ÷ | 5 | = _____ | |
| 5 | ÷ | 5 | = _____ | | 35 | ÷ | 5 | = _____ | |
| 10 | ÷ | 5 | = _____ | | 30 | ÷ | 5 | = _____ | |
| 15 | ÷ | 5 | = _____ | | 35 | ÷ | 5 | = _____ | |
| 20 | ÷ | 5 | = _____ | | 30 | ÷ | 5 | = _____ | |
| 25 | ÷ | 5 | = _____ | | 35 | ÷ | 5 | = _____ | |
| 30 | ÷ | 5 | = _____ | | 30 | ÷ | 5 | = _____ | |

## EXTRA CHALLENGE!

Lady Rebecca's diamonds were stolen. Beside her empty jewelry box was this note!

| | |
|---|---|
| What is full of spades that never shovel? | What is full of hearts that never love? |
| What is full of clubs that never hit a ball? | What is full of diamonds that are never worn? |

Solve the riddle by replacing the answers to the problems with the alphabet code.

| A = 5 | B = 10 | C = 15 | D = 20 | O = 25 | R = 30 | X = 35 |
|---|---|---|---|---|---|---|

5 x 3 = _____    5 x 1 = _____    5 x 6 = _____    5 x 4 = _____    5 x 2 = _____    5 x 5 = _____    5 x 7 = _____

Lady Rebecca's diamonds are hidden in a _____.

*Great Graph Art: Multiplication & Division Scholastic Professional Books*

# HELPING HANDS

**What kind of sea creature would be a big help in the army?**_____

To find out the answer, solve the problems on page 44. Then plot the number pairs and connect the points. The picture you make will help you solve the riddle. (The answer is upside down at the bottom of this page.)

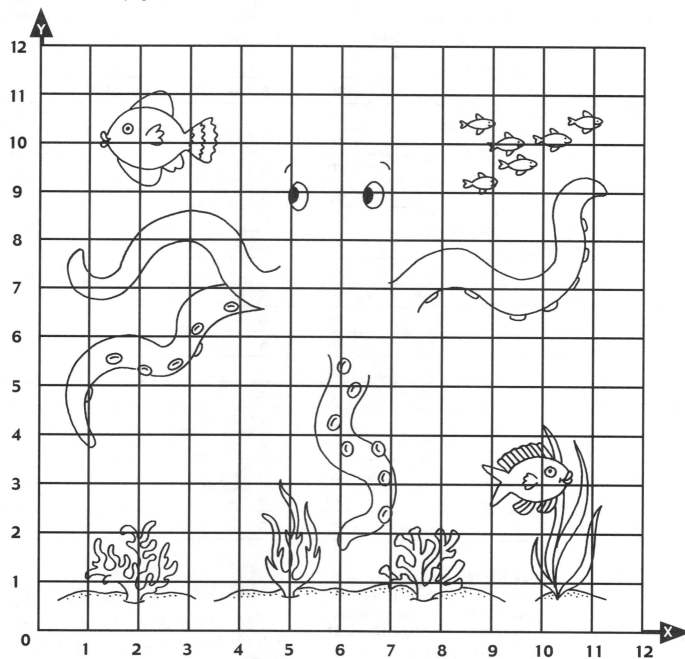

Great Graph Art: Multiplication & Division Scholastic Professional Books

Answer: an octopus

# HELPING HANDS

**1.** Solve each division problem. Example problems have been done for you.

**2.** In the example problems, the numbers **7** and **7** are called a number pair. We write (7, 7).

**3.** Look at the graph on page 43. Graph the number pair in the example. Start at 0.
Go across to the number **7** and up to the number **7**. Plot the point.

**4.** Plot the point for each number pair, in order. Then use a straightedge to connect the points in the order you plotted them. Can you solve the riddle?

| X ⟶ | | | | Y ↑ | | | |
|---|---|---|---|---|---|---|---|
| 35 ÷ 5 = 7 | | | | 35 ÷ 5 = 7 (Example) | | | |
| 40 ÷ 5 = _____ | | | | 45 ÷ 5 = _____ | | | |
| 40 ÷ 5 = _____ | | | | 55 ÷ 5 = _____ | | | |
| 35 ÷ 5 = _____ | | | | 60 ÷ 5 = _____ | | | |
| 25 ÷ 5 = _____ | | | | 60 ÷ 5 = _____ | | | |
| 20 ÷ 5 = _____ | | | | 55 ÷ 5 = _____ | | | |
| 20 ÷ 5 = _____ | | | | 45 ÷ 5 = _____ | | | |
| 25 ÷ 5 = _____ | | | | 35 ÷ 5 = _____ | | | |
| 0 ÷ 5 = _____ | | | | 10 ÷ 5 = _____ | | | |
| 25 ÷ 5 = _____ | | | | 30 ÷ 5 = _____ | | | |
| 15 ÷ 5 = _____ | | | | 0 ÷ 5 = _____ | | | |
| 30 ÷ 5 = _____ | | | | 30 ÷ 5 = _____ | | | |
| 50 ÷ 5 = _____ | | | | 0 ÷ 5 = _____ | | | |
| 35 ÷ 5 = _____ | | | | 30 ÷ 5 = _____ | | | |
| 40 ÷ 5 = _____ | | | | 25 ÷ 5 = _____ | | | |
| 60 ÷ 5 = _____ | | | | 20 ÷ 5 = _____ | | | |
| 40 ÷ 5 = _____ | | | | 30 ÷ 5 = _____ | | | |
| 35 ÷ 5 = _____ | | | | 35 ÷ 5 = _____ | | | |

## EXTRA CHALLENGE!

Oscar the Octopus lost the combination for his treasure chest. All that he has is this note to remind him of the three numbers. Can you figure them out?

Write the three-number combination below:

_____

* All three numbers are different and even.
* The numbers are between 1 and 7.
* The first number is the largest and the last number is the smallest.

Great Graph Art: Multiplication & Division Scholastic Professional Books

# CAMP-OUT

**Why did the baseball pitcher want to go camping?** _____

To find out the answer, solve the problems on page 46. Then plot the number pairs and connect the points. The picture you make will help you solve the riddle. (The answer is upside down at the bottom of this page.)

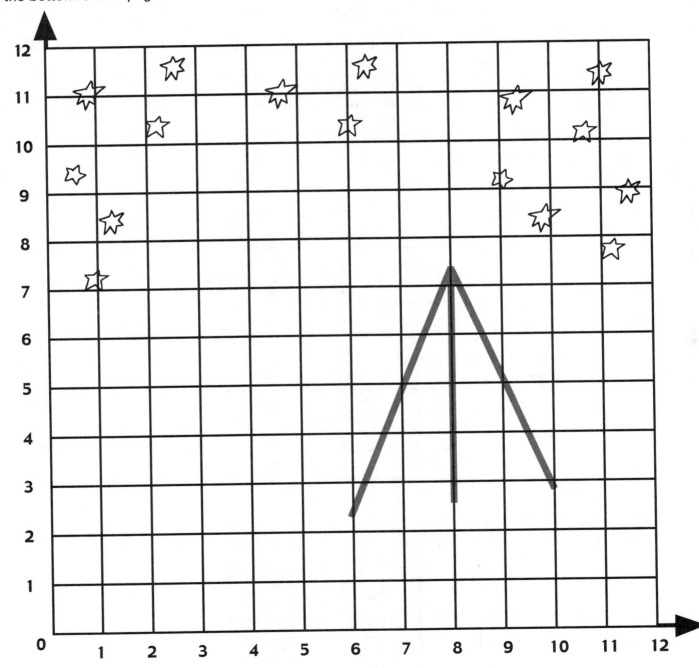

*Great Graph Art: Multiplication & Division Scholastic Professional Books*

Answer: *He liked to pitch tents.*

Name_____

# CAMP-OUT

**1.** Solve each division problem. Example problems have been done for you.

**2.** In the example problems, the numbers **4** and **2** are called a number pair. We write (4, 2).

**3.** Look at the graph on page 45. Graph the number pair in the example. Start at 0.
Go across to the number **4** and up to the number **2**. Plot the point.

**4.** Plot the point for each number pair, in order. Then use a straightedge to connect the points in the order you plotted them. Can you solve the riddle?

X ⟶          Y ⬆

| | | | | | | | |
|---|---|---|---|---|---|---|---|
| 24 ÷ 6 = 4 | | 12 ÷ 6 = 2 (Example) |
| 72 ÷ 6 = ___ | | 18 ÷ 6 = ___ |
| 66 ÷ 6 = ___ | | 30 ÷ 6 = ___ |
| 54 ÷ 6 = ___ | | 48 ÷ 6 = ___ |
| 48 ÷ 6 = ___ | | 60 ÷ 6 = ___ |
| 18 ÷ 6 = ___ | | 60 ÷ 6 = ___ |
| 12 ÷ 6 = ___ | | 48 ÷ 6 = ___ |
| 6 ÷ 6 = ___ | | 36 ÷ 6 = ___ |
| 0 ÷ 6 = ___ | | 24 ÷ 6 = ___ |
| 24 ÷ 6 = ___ | | 12 ÷ 6 = ___ |
| 30 ÷ 6 = ___ | | 24 ÷ 6 = ___ |
| 36 ÷ 6 = ___ | | 36 ÷ 6 = ___ |
| 42 ÷ 6 = ___ | | 48 ÷ 6 = ___ |
| 48 ÷ 6 = ___ | | 60 ÷ 6 = ___ |

## EXTRA CHALLENGE!

Fill in the missing numbers in the white boxes below. Read the problems across and down.

| 42 | ÷ | 7 | = | |
|---|---|---|---|---|
| ÷ | | ÷ | | ÷ |
| 6 | | 1 | | |
| = | | = | | = |
| | ÷ | | = | |

| 24 | ÷ | 6 | = | |
|---|---|---|---|---|
| ÷ | | ÷ | | ÷ |
| 4 | | 1 | | |
| = | | = | | = |
| | ÷ | | = | |

# OUT ON A LIMB

**What has many limbs, but cannot walk?**_____

To find out the answer, solve the problems on page 48. Then plot the number pairs and connect the points. The picture you make will help you solve the riddle. (The answer is upside down at the bottom of this page.)

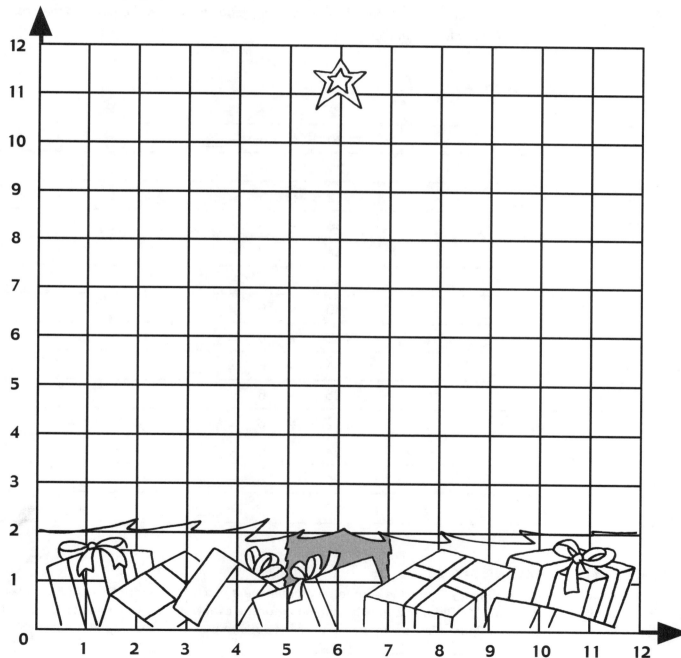

Answer: *a tree*

# OUT ON A LIMB

**1.** Solve each division problem. Example problems have been done for you.

**2.** In the example problems, the numbers **12** and **2** are called a number pair. We write (12, 2).

**3.** Look at the graph on page 47. Graph the number pair in the example. Start at 0.
Go across to the number **12** and up to the number **2**. Plot the point.

**4.** Plot the point for each number pair, in order. Then use a straightedge to connect the points in the order you plotted them. Can you solve the riddle?

X ⟶                                              Y ↑

| | | | | | | | | | |
|---|---|---|---|---|---|---|---|---|---|
| 72 | ÷ | 6 | = | 12 | 12 | ÷ | 6 | = | 2  (Example) |
| 54 | ÷ | 6 | = | _____ | 30 | ÷ | 6 | = | _____ |
| 66 | ÷ | 6 | = | _____ | 24 | ÷ | 6 | = | _____ |
| 48 | ÷ | 6 | = | _____ | 42 | ÷ | 6 | = | _____ |
| 60 | ÷ | 6 | = | _____ | 36 | ÷ | 6 | = | _____ |
| 42 | ÷ | 6 | = | _____ | 54 | ÷ | 6 | = | _____ |
| 54 | ÷ | 6 | = | _____ | 48 | ÷ | 6 | = | _____ |
| 36 | ÷ | 6 | = | _____ | 66 | ÷ | 6 | = | _____ |
| 18 | ÷ | 6 | = | _____ | 48 | ÷ | 6 | = | _____ |
| 30 | ÷ | 6 | = | _____ | 54 | ÷ | 6 | = | _____ |
| 12 | ÷ | 6 | = | _____ | 36 | ÷ | 6 | = | _____ |
| 24 | ÷ | 6 | = | _____ | 42 | ÷ | 6 | = | _____ |
| 6 | ÷ | 6 | = | _____ | 24 | ÷ | 6 | = | _____ |
| 24 | ÷ | 6 | = | _____ | 30 | ÷ | 6 | = | _____ |
| 0 | ÷ | 6 | = | _____ | 12 | ÷ | 6 | = | _____ |

## EXTRA CHALLENGE!

The fifth annual Soda Chugging Contest is sure to be a great event. Each person drinks as many sodas as possible in ten minutes. Mr. Bubb L. Zup is buying soda for the event. He knows he needs 72 cans of soda in all, but he can't figure out how many six-packs of soda to buy. Can you help him out with an answer?_____

*Great Graph Art: Multiplication & Division Scholastic Professional Books*

Name_____

# BIRTHDAY GIFT

**What did the baseball player buy his wife for her birthday?**_____

To find out the answer, solve the problems on page 50. Then plot the number pairs and connect the points. The picture you make will help you solve the riddle. (The answer is upside down at the bottom of this page.)

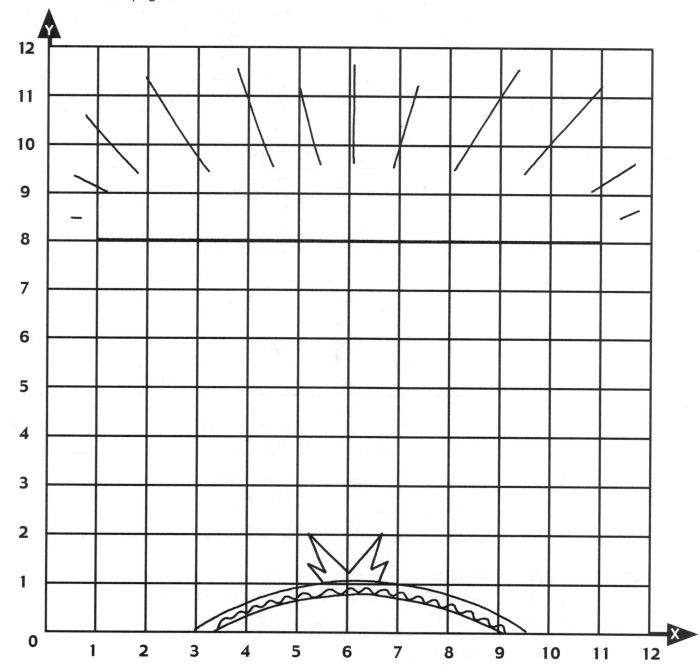

Great Graph Art: Multiplication & Division Scholastic Professional Books

Answer: a diamond

Name_____

# BIRTHDAY GIFT

**1.** Solve each division problem. Example problems have been done for you.

**2.** In the example problems, the numbers **6** and **1** are called a number pair. We write (6,1).

**3.** Look at the graph on page 49. Graph the number pair in the example. Start at 0.
Go across to the number **6** and up to the number **1**. Plot the point.

**4.** Plot the point for each number pair, in order. Then use a straightedge to connect the points in the order
you plotted them. After the word STOP, start a new line. Can you solve the riddle?

**X** ⟶      **Y** ↑

| | |
|---|---|
| $42 \div 7 = 6$ | $7 \div 7 = 1$ (Example) |
| $77 \div 7 = \underline{\hspace{1cm}}$ | $56 \div 7 = \underline{\hspace{1cm}}$ |
| $70 \div 7 = \underline{\hspace{1cm}}$ | $63 \div 7 = \underline{\hspace{1cm}}$ |
| $14 \div 7 = \underline{\hspace{1cm}}$ | $63 \div 7 = \underline{\hspace{1cm}}$ |
| $7 \div 7 = \underline{\hspace{1cm}}$ | $56 \div 7 = \underline{\hspace{1cm}}$ |
| $42 \div 7 = \underline{\hspace{1cm}}$ | $7 \div 7 = \underline{\hspace{1cm}}$ |
| $63 \div 7 = \underline{\hspace{1cm}}$ | $56 \div 7 = \underline{\hspace{1cm}}$ |
| $56 \div 7 = \underline{\hspace{1cm}}$ | $63 \div 7 = \underline{\hspace{1cm}}$ STOP |
| $42 \div 7 = \underline{\hspace{1cm}}$ | $7 \div 7 = \underline{\hspace{1cm}}$ |
| $21 \div 7 = \underline{\hspace{1cm}}$ | $56 \div 7 = \underline{\hspace{1cm}}$ |
| $28 \div 7 = \underline{\hspace{1cm}}$ | $63 \div 7 = \underline{\hspace{1cm}}$ STOP |
| $42 \div 7 = \underline{\hspace{1cm}}$ | $63 \div 7 = \underline{\hspace{1cm}}$ |
| $35 \div 7 = \underline{\hspace{1cm}}$ | $56 \div 7 = \underline{\hspace{1cm}}$ |
| $42 \div 7 = \underline{\hspace{1cm}}$ | $7 \div 7 = \underline{\hspace{1cm}}$ |
| $49 \div 7 = \underline{\hspace{1cm}}$ | $56 \div 7 = \underline{\hspace{1cm}}$ |
| $42 \div 7 = \underline{\hspace{1cm}}$ | $63 \div 7 = \underline{\hspace{1cm}}$ |

## EXTRA CHALLENGE!

Today is Amina's birthday. Use the information below to figure out how old she is.

◆ Today Amina is twice as old as her little brother.

◆ Amina's brother Zack is less than 8 but more than 5 years old.

◆ Both of the children's ages are even numbers.

Amina is _____ years old.

*Great Graph Art: Multiplication & Division Scholastic Professional Books*

**Name**_____

# FAKE STONES

## What do you call an artificial stone?_____

To find out the answer, solve the problems on page 52. Then plot the number pairs and connect the points. The picture you make will help you solve the riddle. (The answer is upside down at the bottom of this page.)

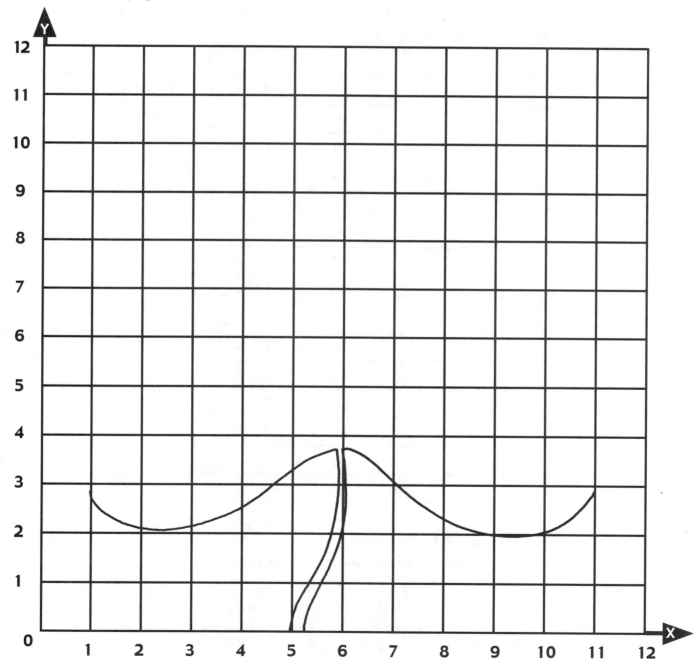

# FAKE STONES

**1.** Solve each division problem. Example problems have been done for you.

**2.** In the example problems, the numbers **11** and **3** are called a number pair. We write (11, 3).

**3.** Look at the graph on page 51. Graph the number pair in the example. Start at 0.
Go across to the number **11** and up to the number **3**. Plot the point.

**4.** Plot the point for each number pair, in order. Then use a straightedge to connect the points in the order you plotted them. Can you solve the riddle?

| X ⟶ | | | | Y ↑ | | | |
|---|---|---|---|---|---|---|---|
| 77 ÷ 7 = 11 | | | | 21 ÷ 7 = 3 (Example) | | | |
| 70 ÷ 7 = _____ | | | | 35 ÷ 7 = _____ | | | |
| 77 ÷ 7 = _____ | | | | 49 ÷ 7 = _____ | | | |
| 70 ÷ 7 = _____ | | | | 56 ÷ 7 = _____ | | | |
| 49 ÷ 7 = _____ | | | | 49 ÷ 7 = _____ | | | |
| 63 ÷ 7 = _____ | | | | 70 ÷ 7 = _____ | | | |
| 56 ÷ 7 = _____ | | | | 77 ÷ 7 = _____ | | | |
| 42 ÷ 7 = _____ | | | | 70 ÷ 7 = _____ | | | |
| 28 ÷ 7 = _____ | | | | 77 ÷ 7 = _____ | | | |
| 21 ÷ 7 = _____ | | | | 70 ÷ 7 = _____ | | | |
| 35 ÷ 7 = _____ | | | | 49 ÷ 7 = _____ | | | |
| 14 ÷ 7 = _____ | | | | 56 ÷ 7 = _____ | | | |
| 7 ÷ 7 = _____ | | | | 49 ÷ 7 = _____ | | | |
| 14 ÷ 7 = _____ | | | | 35 ÷ 7 = _____ | | | |
| 7 ÷ 7 = _____ | | | | 21 ÷ 7 = _____ | | | |

## EXTRA CHALLENGE!

Replace each division problem with the answer and read the message.

> Dear Gold Miner,
>
> If you want (14 ÷ 7) find the (28 ÷ 7 tune), cross (Cot 70 ÷ 7) Creek and climb Twin Peaks.
> Find the abandoned mine. Walk (42 ÷ 7) paces (in 14 ÷ 7) the mine. Look (28 ÷ 7) a hole in the wall.
> The bag of gold is buried (28 ÷ 7) inches deep. You can trust that everything I have said here is true.
>
> Sincerely,
> Ima Liar

*Great Graph Art: Multiplication & Division Scholastic Professional Books*

Name_____

# FRUIT WITH AN ATTITUDE

**What is the crankiest fruit of all?**_____

To find out the answer, solve the problems on page 54. Then plot the number pairs and connect the points. The picture you make will help you solve the riddle. (The answer is upside down at the bottom of this page.)

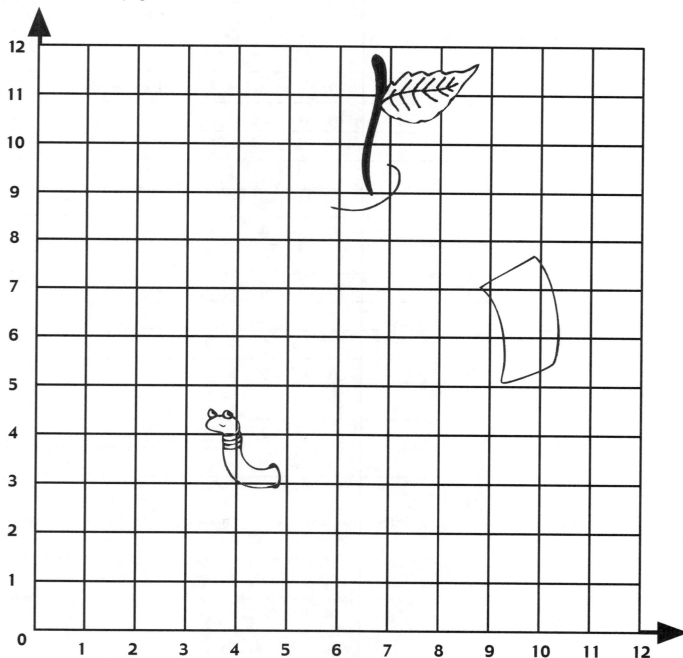

Answer: a crab apple

# FRUIT WITH AN ATTITUDE

**1.** Solve each division problem. Example problems have been done for you.

**2.** In the example problems, the numbers **5** and **1** are called a number pair. We write (5, 1).

**3.** Look at the graph on page 53. Graph the number pairs in the example. Start at 0.
Go across to the number **5** and up to the number **1**. Plot the point.

**4.** Plot the point for each number pair, in order. Then use a straightedge to connect the points in the order
you plotted them. Can you solve the riddle?

X ⟶　　　　　　　　　　　　Y ↑

| | | | | | | | | |
|---|---|---|---|---|---|---|---|---|
| 40 | ÷ | 8 | = | 5 | 8 | ÷ | 8 | = 1　(Example) |
| 48 | ÷ | 8 | = _____ | | 16 | ÷ | 8 | = _____ |
| 56 | ÷ | 8 | = _____ | | 8 | ÷ | 8 | = _____ |
| 72 | ÷ | 8 | = _____ | | 16 | ÷ | 8 | = _____ |
| 88 | ÷ | 8 | = _____ | | 40 | ÷ | 8 | = _____ |
| 88 | ÷ | 8 | = _____ | | 56 | ÷ | 8 | = _____ |
| 80 | ÷ | 8 | = _____ | | 72 | ÷ | 8 | = _____ |
| 56 | ÷ | 8 | = _____ | | 80 | ÷ | 8 | = _____ |
| 40 | ÷ | 8 | = _____ | | 80 | ÷ | 8 | = _____ |
| 24 | ÷ | 8 | = _____ | | 72 | ÷ | 8 | = _____ |
| 16 | ÷ | 8 | = _____ | | 56 | ÷ | 8 | = _____ |
| 16 | ÷ | 8 | = _____ | | 48 | ÷ | 8 | = _____ |
| 24 | ÷ | 8 | = _____ | | 24 | ÷ | 8 | = _____ |
| 40 | ÷ | 8 | = _____ | | 8 | ÷ | 8 | = _____ |

## EXTRA CHALLENGE!

Make a group of caterpillars using the circles below. Use 8 circles to make big caterpillars and 4 circles
to make small caterpillars.

◆ If you make 2 big caterpillars with the circles, how many small caterpillars will you be able to make with
the rest of the circles? _____

◆ If you make 1 big caterpillar with the circles, how many small caterpillars will you be able to make with
the rest of the circles? _____

*Great Graph Art: Multiplication & Division Scholastic Professional Books*

Name_____

# FUNNY MONEY

**I have four quarters but do not equal a dollar. I shine brightly but produce no light. What am I?** _____

To find out the answer, solve the problems on page 56. Then plot the number pairs and connect the points. The picture you make will help you solve the riddle. (The answer is upside down at the bottom of this page.)

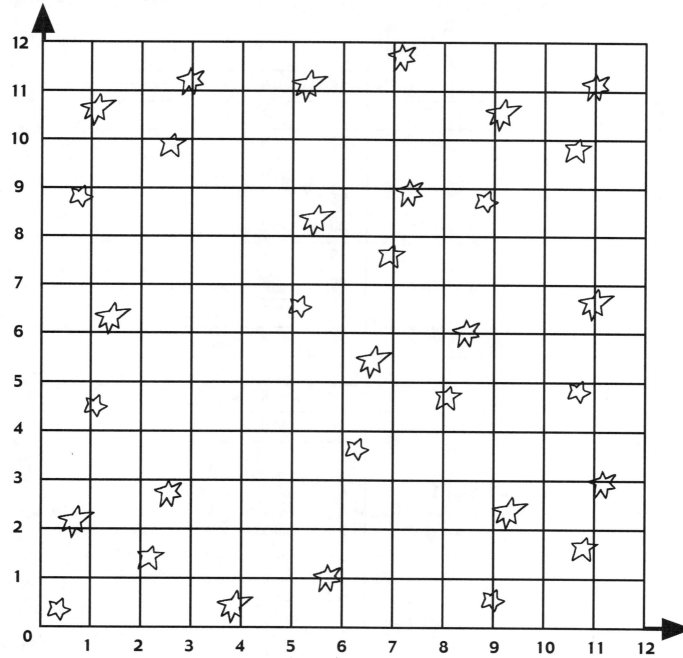

Answer: **the moon**

Name_____

# FUNNY MONEY

**1.** Solve each division problem. Example problems have been done for you.

**2.** In the example problems, the numbers **9** and **2** are called a number pair. We write (9, 2).

**3.** Look at the graph on page 55. Graph the number pair in the example. Start at 0.
Go across to the number **9** and up to the number **2**. Plot the point.

**4.** Plot the point for each number pair, in order. Then use a straightedge to connect the points in the order
you plotted them. Can you solve the riddle?

| X ⟶ | | Y ↑ | |
|---|---|---|---|
| 72 ÷ 8 = 9 | | 16 ÷ 8 = 2 (Example) | |
| 56 ÷ 8 = _____ | | 16 ÷ 8 = _____ | |
| 32 ÷ 8 = _____ | | 40 ÷ 8 = _____ | |
| 32 ÷ 8 = _____ | | 64 ÷ 8 = _____ | |
| 48 ÷ 8 = _____ | | 80 ÷ 8 = _____ | |
| 64 ÷ 8 = _____ | | 80 ÷ 8 = _____ | |
| 48 ÷ 8 = _____ | | 88 ÷ 8 = _____ | |
| 32 ÷ 8 = _____ | | 80 ÷ 8 = _____ | |
| 16 ÷ 8 = _____ | | 64 ÷ 8 = _____ | |
| 16 ÷ 8 = _____ | | 32 ÷ 8 = _____ | |
| 32 ÷ 8 = _____ | | 16 ÷ 8 = _____ | |
| 56 ÷ 8 = _____ | | 8 ÷ 8 = _____ | |
| 72 ÷ 8 = _____ | | 16 ÷ 8 = _____ | |

## EXTRA CHALLENGE!

Solve the problems. Write the answers in words. For example, 16 ÷ 8 = two. Put the answer words
into the correct spaces in the puzzle below. (Hint: There is only one way to solve the puzzle.)

32 ÷ 8 = _____    24 ÷ 8 = _____    40 ÷ 8 = _____    80 ÷ 8 = _____    64 ÷ 8 = _____    16 ÷ 8 = _____

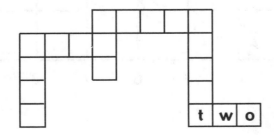

*Great Graph Art: Multiplication & Division Scholastic Professional Books*

# THE SILENT PHONE MYSTERY

**What kind of phone never rings?**_____

To find out the answer, solve the problems on page 58. Then plot the number pairs and connect the points. The picture you make will help you solve the riddle. (The answer is upside down at the bottom of this page.)

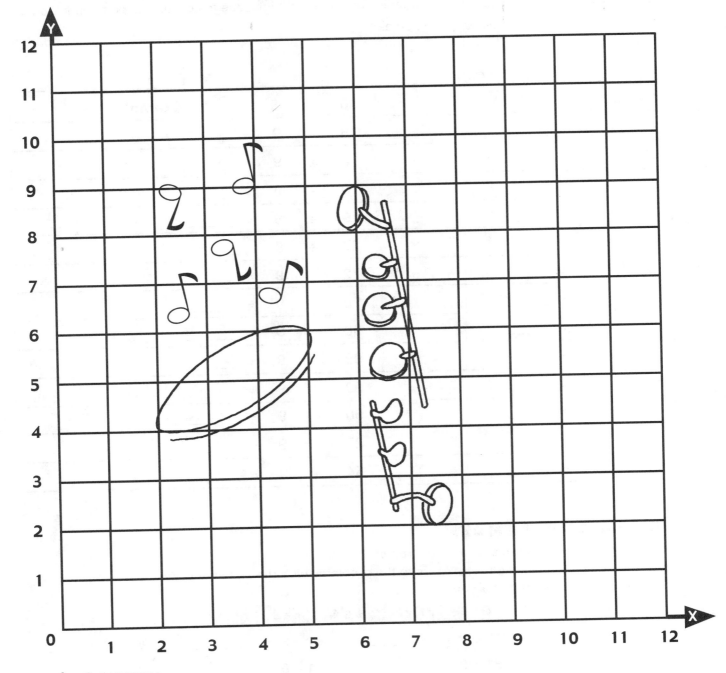

*Great Graph Art: Multiplication & Division Scholastic Professional Books*

Answer: a saxophone

57

# THE SILENT PHONE MYSTERY

**1.** Solve each division problem. Example problems have been done for you.

**2.** In the example problems, the numbers **2** and **4** are called a number pair. We write (2, 4).

**3.** Look at the graph on page 57. Graph the number pair in the example. Start at 0.
Go across to the number **2** and up to the number **4**. Plot the point.

**4.** Plot the point for each number pair, in order. Then use a straightedge to connect the points in the order you plotted them. Can you solve the riddle?

| X → | Y ↑ |
|---|---|
| 18 ÷ 9 = 2 | 36 ÷ 9 = 4 (Example) |
| 36 ÷ 9 = _____ | 18 ÷ 9 = _____ |
| 45 ÷ 9 = _____ | 0 ÷ 9 = _____ |
| 63 ÷ 9 = _____ | 0 ÷ 9 = _____ |
| 72 ÷ 9 = _____ | 9 ÷ 9 = _____ |
| 72 ÷ 9 = _____ | 27 ÷ 9 = _____ |
| 63 ÷ 9 = _____ | 72 ÷ 9 = _____ |
| 63 ÷ 9 = _____ | 90 ÷ 9 = _____ |
| 90 ÷ 9 = _____ | 90 ÷ 9 = _____ |
| 72 ÷ 9 = _____ | 99 ÷ 9 = _____ |
| 54 ÷ 9 = _____ | 99 ÷ 9 = _____ |
| 45 ÷ 9 = _____ | 90 ÷ 9 = _____ |
| 54 ÷ 9 = _____ | 27 ÷ 9 = _____ |
| 45 ÷ 9 = _____ | 54 ÷ 9 = _____ |

## EXTRA CHALLENGE!

What is a German shepherd's favorite instrument?
Solve the riddle by replacing the answers to the problems with the alphabet code.
The first one has been done for you.

| R = 2 | T = 5 | O = 9 | N = 6 | B = 4 | E = 3 | M = 7 |
|---|---|---|---|---|---|---|

45 ÷ 9 = __5__ __T__          18 ÷ 9 = ___ ___          81 ÷ 9 = ___ ___          63 ÷ 9 = ___ ___

36 ÷ 9 = ___ ___          81 ÷ 9 = ___ ___          54 ÷ 9 = ___ ___          27 ÷ 9 = ___ ___

Great Graph Art: Multiplication & Division Scholastic

Name_____

# WHAT AM I?

The older I get, the smaller I become.  What am I?_____

To find out the answer, solve the problems on page 60. Then plot the number pairs and connect the points. The picture you make will help you solve the riddle. (The answer is upside down at the bottom of this page.)

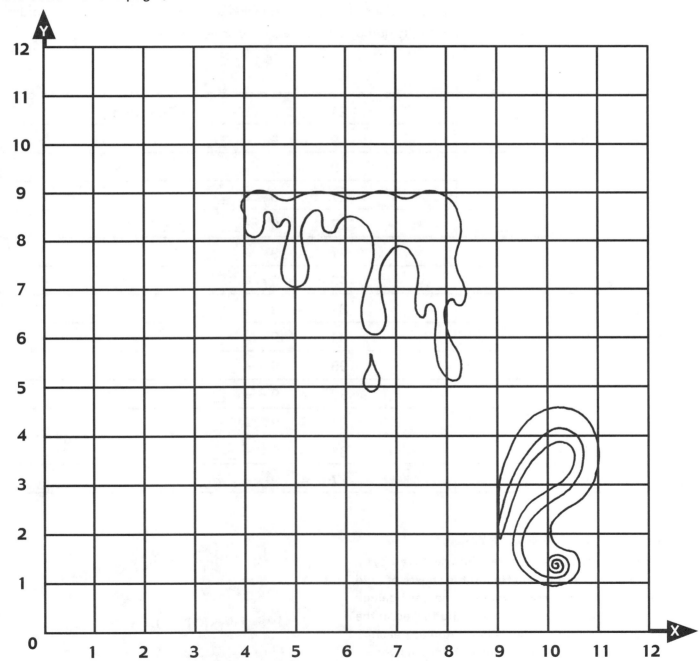

Answer: a candle

Name_____

# WHAT AM I?

**1.** Solve each division problem. Example problems have been done for you.

**2.** In the example problems, the numbers **2** and **3** are called a number pair. We write (2, 3).

**3.** Look at the graph on page 59. Graph the number pair in the example. Start at 0. Go across to the number **2** and up to the number **3**. Plot the point.

**4.** Plot the point for each number pair, in order. Then use a straightedge to connect the points in the order you plotted them. After the word STOP, start a new line. Can you solve the riddle?

X ⟶  Y ↑

| | |
|---|---|
| 18 ÷ 9 = 2 | 27 ÷ 9 = 3 (Example) |
| 36 ÷ 9 = _____ | 9 ÷ 9 = _____ |
| 81 ÷ 9 = _____ | 9 ÷ 9 = _____ |
| 81 ÷ 9 = _____ | 27 ÷ 9 = _____ |
| 18 ÷ 9 = _____ | 27 ÷ 9 = _____ STOP |
| 72 ÷ 9 = _____ | 27 ÷ 9 = _____ |
| 72 ÷ 9 = _____ | 45 ÷ 9 = _____ |
| 72 ÷ 9 = _____ | 81 ÷ 9 = _____ |
| 54 ÷ 9 = _____ | 81 ÷ 9 = _____ |
| 54 ÷ 9 = _____ | 99 ÷ 9 = _____ |
| 63 ÷ 9 = _____ | 90 ÷ 9 = _____ |
| 54 ÷ 9 = _____ | 81 ÷ 9 = _____ |
| 36 ÷ 9 = _____ | 81 ÷ 9 = _____ |
| 36 ÷ 9 = _____ | 27 ÷ 9 = _____ |

## EXTRA CHALLENGE!

Captain Crook was a pirate who was loved by none and feared by all. He hid his chests of gold, silver, and jewels somewhere in the Caribbean. When he died, this note was found tucked in the bottom of Captain Crook's boot. Replace each division problem in the note with the answer and read the message.

The (36 ÷ 9 tune) is aboard the ship called (36 ÷ 9 got 90 ÷ 9) Bounty in Red Hook Bay!

Great Graph Art: Multiplication & Division Scholastic Professional Books

# ANSWERS  *Completed graphs and answers for Extra Challenge! questions*

Pages 5–6: **Cat Detective**

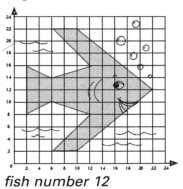

*fish number 12*

Pages 7–8: **Cupid's Visit**

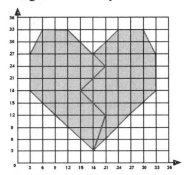

*6 pieces of candy*

Pages 9–10: **Pet Store**

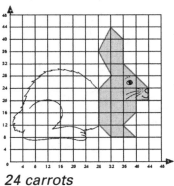

*24 carrots*

Pages 11–12: **Alphabet**

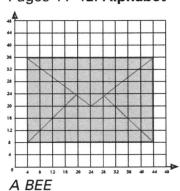

*A BEE*

Pages 13–14: **Outer Space**

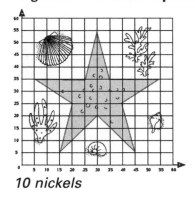

*10 nickels*

Pages 15–16: **Coyote by Moonligh**t

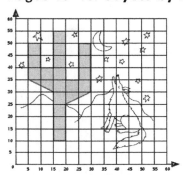

*HE WAS ALWAYS HORSING AROUND.*

Pages 17–18: **The Mermaid Teacher**

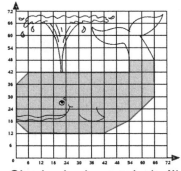

*She had a long tale (tail).*

Pages 19–20: **A Trip to the Dentist**

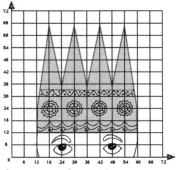

*bag number 12*

## Pages 21–22: **Up, Up, and Away**

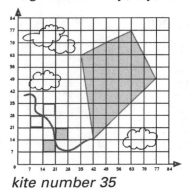

*kite number 35*

## Pages 23–24: **Math Test**

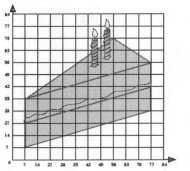

*a. 3 and 7   b. 9 and 9   c. 4 and 7*

## Pages 25–26: **Letters and Flowers**

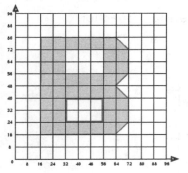

| 8 | x | 1 | 8 |
|---|---|---|---|
| x |   | x | x |
| 1 | x | 4 | 4 |
| 8 | x | 4 | 32 |

| 6 | x | 2 | 12 |
|---|---|---|---|
| X |   | x | x |
| 2 | x | 4 | 8 |
| 12 | x | 8 | 96 |

## Pages 27–28: **Home Sweet Home**

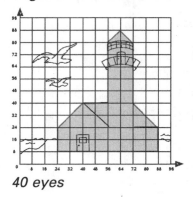

*40 eyes*

## Pages 29–30: **Boat Shopping**

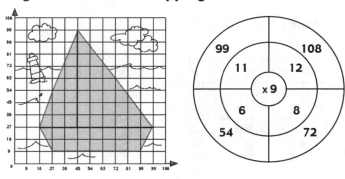

## Pages 31–32: **Locked Coffin**

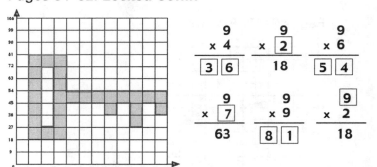

$$\begin{array}{r} 9 \\ \times\, 4 \\ \hline \boxed{3}\,\boxed{6} \end{array} \qquad \begin{array}{r} 9 \\ \times\, \boxed{2} \\ \hline 18 \end{array} \qquad \begin{array}{r} 9 \\ \times\, 6 \\ \hline \boxed{5}\,\boxed{4} \end{array}$$

$$\begin{array}{r} 9 \\ \times\, \boxed{7} \\ \hline 63 \end{array} \qquad \begin{array}{r} 9 \\ \times\, 9 \\ \hline \boxed{8}\,\boxed{1} \end{array} \qquad \begin{array}{r} \boxed{9} \\ \times\, 2 \\ \hline 18 \end{array}$$

## Pages 33–34: **Touchdown**

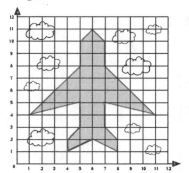

*The winning cereal box is number 148.*

## Pages 35–36: Flying Butter

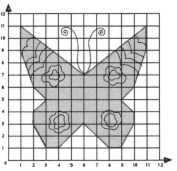

*5 groups of cows*

## Pages 37–38: Ring! Ring!

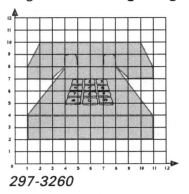

*297-3260*

## Pages 39–40: Bird of Peace

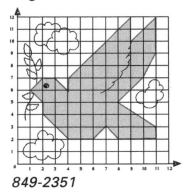

*849-2351*

## Pages 41–42: King John

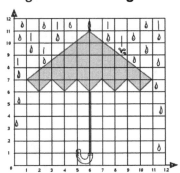

*Lady Rebecca's diamonds are hidden in a CARD BOX.*

## Pages 43–44: Helping Hands

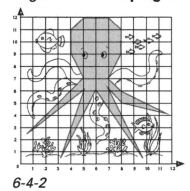

*6-4-2*

## Pages 45–46: Camp-Out

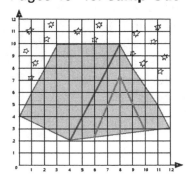

| 42 | ÷ | 7 | = | 6 |
|----|---|---|---|---|
| ÷ |  | ÷ |  | ÷ |
| 6 |  | 1 |  | 6 |
| = |  | = |  | = |
| 7 | ÷ | 7 | = | 1 |

| 24 | ÷ | 6 | = | 4 |
|----|---|---|---|---|
| ÷ |  | ÷ |  | ÷ |
| 4 |  | 1 |  | 4 |
| = |  | = |  | = |
| 6 | ÷ | 6 | = | 1 |

## Pages 47–48: Out on a Limb

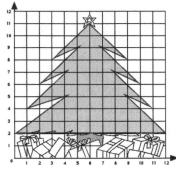

*12 six-packs of soda*

## Pages 49–50: Birthday Gift

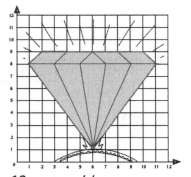

*12 years old*

## Pages 51–52: Fake Stones

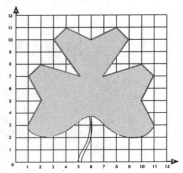

Dear Gold Miner,

If you want *two* find the *four*tune, cross Cot*ten* Creek and climb Twin Peaks. Find the abandoned mine. Walk *six* paces in*two* the mine. Look *four* a hole in the wall. The bag of gold is buried *four* inches deep. You can trust that everything I have said here is true.

Sincerely,
Ima Liar

## Pages 53–54: Fruit With an Attitude

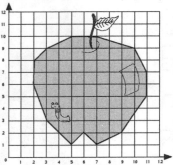

*1 small caterpillar; 3 small caterpillars*

## Pages 55–56: Funny Money

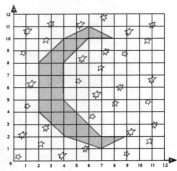

## Pages 57–58: The Silent Phone Mystery

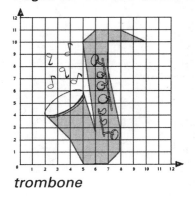

*trombone*

## Pages 59–60: What Am I?

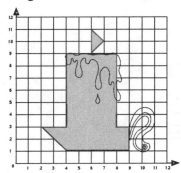

The *four*tune is aboard a ship called *four*got*ten* Bounty in Red Hook Bay!

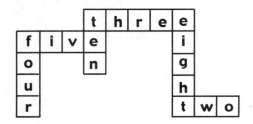